PLEASE
LIE TO ME

PLEASE
LIE TO ME

Thompson Barton
with Don White

Goatboy Press
Ashland, Oregon

Cover design: Kostis Pavlou
Interior design: Christy Collins, Constellation Book Services

ISBN: 978-0-692-99697-3

Printed in the United States of America

Library of Congress Control Number: 2018939701

Contents

PART III – Accountable Consciousness

Our Mission:

An accountably conscious world

Foreword

In 1996, I became CEO of an ophthalmology clinic with a legacy stretching back to 1911. My dozen years' experience in healthcare administration had scarcely prepared me for the surprises I would encounter.

Three years in, I hated the results I was getting. I was dismayed to discover this small clinic was beset by many of the same ills as larger health care organizations. People gossiped about coworkers behind their backs. People said "Yes" when they meant "No." Meetings were little more than tiresome posturing and long speeches. People sat on their hands, nodded, and waited for the real meetings that happened afterward in the parking lot. The owners didn't trust each other.

Despite excellent equipment and highly competent doctors and staff, it wasn't a fun place to work. Changes took eons. Resistance was subtle and pervasive. We had a robust Ain't It Awful Club. Humor was used to cut people down; it was difficult to decipher the sarcasm from genuine responses.

I felt outgunned and overwhelmed. I had a vision of the kind of workplace I wanted but what I was doing (and, as it turned out, not doing) wasn't getting us there.

At the time, I was on the board of my children's private school, as was Thompson Barton, who was serving in the role of ombudsman to help diffuse the tension between staff and parents.

As I watched Thompson facilitate board meetings, I felt both anxious and fascinated. He was direct and immediate. I was a card-carrying People Pleaser, and I had plenty of company in my group. Whatever this guy was, he wasn't a member. He said what no one else in the room would say but everyone seemed to be thinking. He had no regard for "politically correct" notions or "comfort zones." With him present, no one got to hide or pretend, which illuminated everything. The real problems and strategic agendas became painfully obvious, and the exposure gave us clarity along with our best chance to do something about them. He never mentioned the name of his methodology during these meetings. He just applied it.

After the resolution of one particularly difficult issue, I remember him quipping, "Real problems get solved when the people solving them get real." That statement gnawed at me for days. I couldn't shake it.

Not long after, I hired Thompson, whom I learned had been practicing Accountable Communication Technology (ACT). Nothing has been the same at our clinic since.

Nearly two decades later, the list of what's changed is too long to recount. Here are a few examples:

- We are fierce in making and keeping detailed agreements.
- We expect them to be kept. This results in far fewer dropped balls.
- We don't sit around wondering what is being said, meant, or implied. We ask about it immediately. For example, "It looks to me like you aren't really saying 'Yes'. Is that so?"
- We have a fraction of the triangulation we previously had. Managers don't waste time running shuttle diplomacy between factions.
- Meetings are about problem-solving. Everyone owns the quality—not just the meeting chair. It is common to hear comments like "Seems like we are

off topic"; "Let's have just one conversation at a time … let her finish"; "You aren't listening to one another"; and "It seems to me we are complete—anybody have anything else to say?"

- We are alert to blaming and quickly turn it toward accountable problem solving. We examine what each person did or didn't do that contributed to whatever situation we are facing. We do not entertain the victim stance.

- We don't pretend we don't notice feuding. It becomes a team responsibility because everyone is affected and has a role in making it better. We address it and expect everyone will engage in problem solving and rebuilding eroded trust.

- We see feedback as a gift and celebrate and reward those who seek it out. "What is your experience of my work and me?" is something employees expect to hear from one another.

- We notice our own and others' defensive behavior and address it immediately. Our goal is to reduce the business cost of defensive behavior.

In 2014, we hired nine more doctors. This was a huge onboarding challenge for the clinical leaders and associated staff. At the joint doctor/manager retreat in 2015, the managers questioned the new doctors' commitment to the culture. The managers felt a protective ownership for it. They feared the new doctors did not appreciate and were not inclined to do what it takes to sustain their cherished culture. Accountability was the unique bedrock of their morale and job satisfaction—so much so they were willing to confront their new bosses about it. That's accountability. This was about their working conditions, and it wasn't negotiable. They were owning the continuity they wanted to see carried from the retiring senior doctors to the new guard. Individual competency with ACT is part of each employee's professional performance evaluation, and they see the doctors as no exception. I felt so proud of everyone as I participated in this meeting. Empowered, our employees do not resort to voting with their feet.

We often lose staff when a spouse finds a job elsewhere. Occasionally, they leave for what looks like a better opportunity. After we implemented ACT, some of those staff later returned, saying they could not tolerate the "business as usual" cultures they experienced everywhere else. More than once I have heard, "You've ruined me—I can't work anywhere else." In 2016, we counted the number who had left and later returned. That percentage was 17 percent of our 140 staff members.

At the end of our last owner retreat, our newest ophthalmologist said he initially chose to join our practice for typical business reasons. After experiencing our culture, he cites that as the reason he expects to be here his entire career.

We often receive unsolicited comments from patients and vendors saying our Medical Eye Clinic staff work together seamlessly and exude a positive attitude.

We have used the services of a highly experienced marketing and general business consultant for more than twenty years. The author of eight books on ophthalmology and leadership, he has observed thousands of ophthalmology practices around the world. About eight years into our adoption of ACT, he wrote, "This is the finest example of organizational transformation I have seen in thirty years."

My early frustrations have vanished. Our clinic is not the same place to work as it was when I first started. We transformed "business as usual" to a culture of true, comprehensive accountability. We are now in the ongoing vigilance phase required for lifelong sustainability.

Ophthalmology and optometry are all about maximizing the quality of our eyesight. That's the whole purpose. Vision allows us to function in our seen world; and the more acute, the better. I have come to believe having keen *insight* is an equally critical faculty. Awareness reveals what is happening beneath the surface in ourselves as well as one another. ACT is designed to develop awareness skills. As with external seeing, our degree of insight gives access to otherwise obscure information, without which we are blind to what is occurring within our coworkers and ourselves. If people problems go undetected, they go unresolved. It's as simple as that. The collective acuity of our employees' awareness is an invaluable asset to our business. Add to that awareness the courage to address issues openly and with accountability, and we have a workplace that rocks.

Thompson Barton and Don White offer organizational transformation; nothing less. Their work is in a class of its own. And they, too, are in a class of their own. They miss nothing. They truly walk their talk.

As you read this book, you will realize the journey is demanding. If you're "all in," though, I assure you it is absolutely worth the effort and resources.

I look forward to hearing about your journey with Accountable Communication Technology.

Keith Casebolt, CEO Medical Eye Center
Medford, Oregon

Preface

I am a recovering liar and blamer in a society awash with pretending and blaming. I specialize in transforming organizations from this costly and pervasive mayhem to Accountable Consciousness.

I would never have guessed this journey would begin with tennis.

Among other endeavors, I played and taught tennis for forty years. In 1977, I discovered *The Inner Game of Tennis*, by Tim Gallwey. After reading the first few pages, I was already on the phone enrolling in his next available workshop. Finally, someone had discovered a way to consciously access the hallowed but elusive "zone"—in which anyone continually plays at their very best!

I found Tim was as brilliant in person as in print.

In tennis, you enter the zone by focusing all your attention on one experience alone: seeing the tennis ball at the exclusion of all potential distractions (far different from merely "watching" the ball).

Tim taught us to regard the ball as a mandala and tennis as a meditation. This creates a single-minded focus in which you are visually glued to the ball as if hypnotized (even glancing at the other player will cause a visual disconnection with the ball). Seeing in this way creates an intense connection to the present moment. It results in a beautiful optimization and coordination of mind and body. I finally performed at my absolute best—for seven days straight!

I came away from that week feeling liberated. Thanks to Tim's Inner Game techniques, I now possessed the antidote for performance anxiety—both on and off the tennis court.

Tim explained that how we approached, regarded, and played tennis is a metaphor for how we live our lives. Our Image Management Department fouls up our tennis game the same way it fouls up our lives. It clutters our mind with fears about screwing up and being seen as a lousy player, triggering embarrassment and humiliation.

The Inner Game has since guided my life. I still feel the impact of being immersed in the Inner Game during that transformative week.

A year later, I was coaching the tennis team at an Oregon community college and teaching Inner Game courses which I created for the Physical Education Department. Having discovered how to apply the Inner Game to other sports, I became the Inner Game coach for the college teams. Tim Gallwey's book *The Inner Game of Skiing* was well received by our outstanding ski team in Bend, Oregon.

My dream career soon became obvious: keep doing this. I focused on my next step: obtaining my master of arts degree.

During the 1970s, Holism was gaining attention. I found myself drawn to the mind-body-spirit movement. Researching potential graduate schools, I came across a master of arts in holistic psychology offered by Antioch University West at its San Francisco satellite campus. I was excited to discover many of my favorite authors were on the faculty, including George Leonard (author of *The Ultimate Athlete*), Michael Murphy (co-founder of the Esalen Institute and author of *The Psychic Side of Sports*, my all-time favorite book about the zone). As if that weren't enough, I noticed that Bob Kriegel—who had coauthored *The Inner Game of Skiing* with Tim Gallwey—was teaching in the program. Where do I sign up?

In September of 1979, I found myself sitting across from Will Schutz, PhD, founder of this nascent holistic psychology program. Each incoming student had a thirty-minute interview with him as part of orientation. Mine was late that afternoon. Filled with anticipation, I gushed about the program. He listened, never breaking eye contact, commenting occasionally. We sat facing each other on two chairs—the only furniture in the spacious room. At one point, I noticed the light was fading. I felt certain he, too, was aware of the growing dimness. We didn't mention it. We continued. Eventually, we were sitting in the dark, saying little. This man was not afraid of the dark—or silence. I liked that. I liked him. It was the beginning of a bond, and Will's seminal impact on my life.

I was fascinated to learn that Dr. Schutz was teaching how to achieve and enjoy extraordinary human relationships in organizations, using the same profound approach that Tim Gallwey was using for tennis and life. I knew it worked in tennis, but in business organizations—really?

Yes, as it turns out. Thirty-seven years of "Yes."

Dr. Schutz regarded three fundamental principles as essential for vibrant aliveness of body, mind, and spirit: 1) be truthful with others, 2) take full responsibility for your life, and 3) be self-aware. I thought I was advanced in each, having studied these subjects and attended related seminars and workshops for years. Early feedback from my fellow students and faculty, however, revealed a different story. My ego underwent a seismic jolt.

I soon found being truly open, aware, and self-responsible was disorienting and disarming. "Openness" was about transparency—not "brutal honesty." Given how I was raised, pretending and blaming came naturally to me. How could I give up the seeming protection afforded me by these well-developed defense mechanisms?

My ego's Image Management Department panicked. I felt like I was going through "cold turkey" withdrawal.

I had a decision to make. Was I committed to being cool—or to being real? My ego was committed to looking good, but I was irresistibly attracted to being real.

I became captivated by what I experienced in a community of people committed to being truthful and taking full responsibility for themselves. There was no bull-shitting or blaming allowed. To varying degrees, my fellow students were also going through re-programing. All of us were recovering liars and blamers.

We learned that our defenses such as self-deception, withholding, pretending, and blaming came from internal insecurities and were not caused by other people. In this high-feedback, no-victim, integrity-focused community, my self-awareness inexorably grew. The more I immersed myself in this new reality, the more my Image Management Department faded into the background. I became less ego-driven.

When I first enrolled in the MA program, I was keen to return to my teaching position. I sped through the program in two years. I soon realized this experience was life-changing, however. I was tasting the self-empowerment, self-respect and freedom that come from being real and assuming complete responsibility for every moment of my life. My career was on a new trajectory.

Since this was the most galvanizing experience of my life, I decided to stay seven more years to apprentice with Will. During this time, I took the opportunity to become adjunct faculty and teach Inner Game courses in the MA program.

Called "The Human Element," Dr. Schutz's five-day workshop, designed for business organizations and corporations, was also used by the military and NASA. I witnessed how his methodology and interventions restored trust and dismembered the traditional blame game, resulting in previously unattainable efficiencies and business success for his clients.

During a Human Element workshop for Procter & Gamble in 1985, I met Don White, the manager who brought in Dr. Schutz. Over the next few years, I often worked with Don and his groups. The results he achieved by applying The Human Element at his manufacturing facility were epic by any measure.

Don is a pillar of accountability and integrity. He has the unflinching courage required to live both and is an ongoing source of inspiration for me. I am grateful for him as a colleague and beloved friend, and for his collaboration on this book.

In 1991, Don and I founded an organizational transformation firm named Barton White Associates. We created Accountable Communication Technology (ACT) from our work with The Human Element and Don's twenty-seven years of management experience at Procter & Gamble.

It is deeply satisfying to witness the cultural and organizational metamorphosis that occurs when the practice of Accountable Consciousness supplants fear and the blame and mistrust that feed on it.

April 2018
Thompson Barton
Ashland, Oregon

Introduction

I will never forget what happened many years ago during the opening session of an Accountable Communication Technology (ACT) workshop. Don, my co-facilitator, asked the attendees how important trust was to their productivity and business success.

After a long, awkward silence in the room a long-time employee, arms folded tightly, blurted out: "Well, it can't be that important because I know nobody in this room trusts anybody else, and this company has been in business for more than sixty years."

In other words, "Why bother?"

For almost forty years I have witnessed a kind of suffering so pervasive it's like a plague. The affliction is chronic. Once afflicted, the host becomes withdrawn and guarded. The common belief is that there is nothing to be done about it. Resigned, the afflicted will tell you that "It's just how it is" and to "just get used to it."

The affliction is Mistrust. And it is highly contagious.

Collectively, it defines the morale and productivity of an organization. This is known as "business as usual."

But it is not fate, and the ongoing suffering is unnecessary. I feel sad for all those afflicted and for their organizations. Most people will spend their entire work life unaware it could be otherwise. It is in an effort to relieve this needless suffering that I write this book.

In 1984, Will Schutz, PhD, published *The Truth Option*. In the Introduction, he notes: "Machiavelli survives as the most profound influence on human interaction. If a country's negotiations are marked by deception . . . it may be because that is the way its people deal with each other. Public policy is related directly to private affairs. If a nation spends half its energies on national defense, it is probably because that is the amount of energy its people spend on private defensiveness."

The word "Option" in the title suggests that we will not be truthful without intentionally choosing to be. Our default position is always closed rather than open. We are nowhere near as open as we like to think we are. We are suspicious of one another as a result of our training and socialization. A statement like "Honesty is the best policy" is held as an ideal, yet always dismissed as impractical when weighed against our belief— rarely, if ever, challenged—about its potential for disastrous consequences. The fear engendered by that belief overrides moral directives such as "You should be open and honest," "Never tell a lie," "Treat others as you want to be treated."

An organization is as toxic as its secrets

In 2008, Stephen M.R. Covey published *The Speed of Trust* with the subtitle *The One Thing That Changes Everything*. The book was widely praised by executives and leaders of many of the largest corporations in the world. The first twenty-six pages are filled with thorough research and data that establish the extraordinary business value of being trustworthy, and the cost of breeches of trust, internally and publicly. In spite of the extensive business proof Covey offers, deception-as-usual continues across the globe to this day, unfazed. Volkswagen, Wells Fargo; the examples go on and on.

If trust is so important as a business asset—which almost all business owners and leaders claim—why is it still so rare in organizations?

Because the problem is not a trust issue; the problem is fear.

That's what this book is about.

Please Lie to Me makes unflinching eye contact with fear.

Please Lie to Me defines what it takes to liberate you, your workforce, and your organization from being hostage to fear.

Please Lie to Me takes on fear in the workplace by using a new agreement to replace business as usual. Implementing this New Agreement establishes Accountable Consciousness, which transforms the culture and the business.

Your company values are the sum of all employees' attitudes and behavior at any given time.

By following the principles in *Please Lie to Me*, business owners and leaders will finally take back control of their cultures and organizations. In so doing, employees become fully engaged and the organization will reach currently unattainable heights of effectiveness and productivity.

> *Make no mistake about it: whoever is responsible to oversee and lead such a transformation must be an individual who acknowledges and understands both the impact of fear in the workplace and the way past it. This requires a person with passion, grit, pit-bull determination, and unflagging commitment to the process. These individuals are rare. They cannot be assigned this task; these individuals must be found.* –Don White

After twenty-seven years of working directly with business organizations I have yet to meet a leader or owner who, once realizing how much the lack of accountability and trust are costing the company, did not commit to transforming their organization.

Is this inspiring or threatening to you?

• • •

Part I of this book deals with our fear of one another, and The Usual Agreement that rules all of our relationships by default until we choose to do something about it.

Part II is The New Agreement. It describes what it takes to build trust with coworkers using Accountable Communication Technology (ACT).

Part III describes Accountable Consciousness and what it means to live accordingly. It is the source of self-empowerment, self-respect, integrity, and effectiveness.

If I am not determined to be open and honest with you, as well as insistent that you be open and honest with me, by default we are agreeing to its opposite. Hence the title of this book: *Please Lie to Me.*

This agreement is informal and non-verbal, and we are not even aware this is happening.

PART I

THE USUAL AGREEMENT

The Usual Agreement

If awareness, openness, and accountability aren't the norm, what is "normal" in the workplace?

This is:

- I won't ask you what you are withholding if you won't ask me what I am withholding.
- I won't say what I see if you won't say what you see. I won't ask you what you see if you won't ask me what I see.
- I won't say what I am thinking if you won't say what you're thinking. I won't ask you what you are really thinking if you won't ask me.
- I won't say what I'm sensing if you won't say what you're sensing. I won't ask you what you are sensing if you won't ask me.
- I won't say what I'm wondering if you won't, and I won't ask you what you are wondering if you won't ask me.
- I won't ask you what you really mean if you won't ask me what I really mean.
- I won't say what I am really feeling if you won't say what you're really feeling. I won't ask you what you are really feeling if you won't ask me.
- I won't say what I want if you won't say what you really want. I won't ask you what you really want if you won't ask me.
- I won't question you if you won't question me.

- I won't be direct with you if you won't be direct with me.
- I won't put you on the spot if you won't put me on the spot.

The Usual Agreement is the way we normalize and institutionalize pretending.

Why do we do this?

Fear

By and large, we don't trust one another.

This is no one's fault and everyone's problem.

How long does it take for someone to get to know you?

"It depends," right?

On what?

What does it take for you to "let your guard down"?

What is it that you are guarding?

From what and from whom are you protecting yourself?

Most of us are chronically afraid of one another.

Don't think so?

Notice how often you withhold and pretend today.

If you're not afraid, why are you hiding?

You may not even notice this about yourself. It's not flattering.

"I'm a liar" T-shirts don't sell well. Neither do shirts that say "I'm afraid."

You tell yourself that you would be open and honest with others if they could handle it, but they can't, so you spare them. *(The truth is you are afraid of their reactions and of dealing with them.)*

Which is exactly how they justify lying to you.

But you *hate* being lied to.

It's like being ripped off, somehow. You feel disrespected and hurt. Violated. Abused. Trust evaporates, and wounds with a long half-life are formed.

And yet, we continue to lie to one another like addicts, scared to death of being straight up, of being real.

What are the consequences of this in the workplace and to the business?

Notice how much time we spend carefully watching one another and trying to "read between the lines." Especially in meetings.

Most people see and know what is going on. Most people say nothing.

There is no such thing as a "hidden agenda." Everybody knows what's going on. It's collusion; the group Pretend is the "elephant" in the room. Discussions go in circles because no one is being straight. It takes a long time to avoid saying something . . .

Jack Welch, CEO of General Electric for forty years, notes in his 2005 book *Winning*, "They [senior managers] withhold in order to make people feel better or to avoid conflict and sugar coat to maintain appearances . . . That's all lack of candor, and is absolutely damaging. And yet, lack of candor permeates almost every aspect of business."

Company values and therefore culture are the sum of all employees' attitudes and behavior at any given time.

Think about your workplace. Consider how much pretending is going on right now, today . . .

What Do You Pretend?

From the front of the hotel meeting room I watch as a work-group of twenty-four people from a Midwest US manufacturing facility anxiously self-select into groups of six, configure their chairs into circles, and await the next instruction. After they quiet down, I ask one person in each of the groups to volunteer to go first. I then explain how the activity is to proceed, which results in a few moans followed by a contracted silence in the room.

As frequently happens when I lead this activity, I flash back to my first experience as a participant. I was a new student in the holistic psychology MA program, and this was the first day of classes, 1979. The activity, called "I Pretend," went like this: Sitting in a circle with several other students, the person who had volunteered to start turns to the person to their left and asked "What do you pretend?" The response might be "I pretend to be familiar with books I haven't even heard of before," or "I pretend to be interested in a client when I'm really bored," or "I pretend I'm not competitive around other psychologists." Then the person who just answered turns to the person on their left and asks, "What do you pretend?" After giving an answer, that person turns to the person on their left and asks "What do you pretend?" and this exchange continues around and around the circle. No comment or discussion is permitted.

My experience quickly went from novel to unsettling to unnerving. We did this for thirty minutes, which at agonizing point felt like a lifetime. I had never felt mpletely and relentlessly exposed, found out. Always performance-driven and competitive, I was both puzzled and irritated by others in our group who seemed less anxious and more easily forthcoming with information that would be too embarrassing for me, such as one student's response, "I pretend I don't have a drinking problem," and another's, "I pretend I like my children equally." I was unwilling to acknowledge that I was judgmental and that I thought I was better than most other people.

I dreaded my turn. Frequently I drew a blank, literally at a loss for words. "Why is all this so hard for me?" I wondered, as I stewed in the heavy silence of the group, all eyes on me, waiting. I wanted desperately to explain myself somehow or another, but one ground rule of the activity was to say nothing other than your Pretend. Even though I could identify with others' Pretends, I became flustered and struggled to come up with mine, which often felt superficial, like "I pretend to like disco music."

I was not really paying attention to myself and all that I pretend because I was focused outward on the group's impression and opinion of me, and feared that to say what I pretended would expose me as phony and insecure. My ego would have no part of that! Deep down I believed I was a phony, which plagued me. I certainly did not want to give others the opportunity to be disgusted with me, as well. I had just met these people and was slated to spend the next two years with them.

However, I would not have guessed what evolved within the group as everyone continued to ante-up Pretends that were increasingly personal, real, and revealing: compassion. I could feel it settling over the room. Unspoken, the body language and tone in the group conveyed it. Compassion and respect had emerged, rather than shame and judgment, because it was obvious that *everyone* in the group pretended plenty. Most Pretends were universal, but being open about them took courage. I could stop holding my breath. This would not be Judgment Day. It would be wakeup day. A recovery group was being born. I could come out from hiding in the shadows of shame.

35 Common "Pretends" in the Workplace

Pretending is acting as if you do not think or feel something that you are aware is actually true for you. It's a deception, and a very common defense strategy. Pretending, as with all defenses, is used to avoid feelings of insignificance, incompetence, and being unlikeable.

Over almost forty years, I have witnessed thousands of people participate in the "I Pretend" activity. The range of Pretends include:

I pretend to not be worried about next quarter's results

I pretend we don't put production goals ahead of safety goals

I pretend the new I.T. system is going to work

I pretend to not be mad at people who come late to meetings

I pretend to have confidence in our new team configuration

I pretend to trust headquarters

I pretend there is no us-and-them in the company

I pretend we treat customers the same

I pretend the sales people don't lie to customers about ship dates

I pretend there is no favoritism here

I pretend there is no nepotism here

I pretend I make a difference in my role

I pretend I'm okay with being passed over again

I pretend we can satisfy all our customers

I pretend I'm not over-qualified for my job

I pretend to trust the offshore suppliers

I pretend we aren't still understaffed

I pretend I don't mind being on the road all the time

I pretend our margins are realistic

I pretend the managers don't irritate the hell out of me

I pretend we are going to have a banner year

I pretend the company values mean anything

I pretend the owners care about us

I pretend our products aren't inferior

I pretend I work hard all the time

I pretend to respect the union

I pretend the company vision isn't a joke

I pretend to respect the company

I pretend our budget is realistic

I pretend to trust the board

I pretend to trust people here

I pretend lack of recognition doesn't bother me

I pretend people give me honest feedback

I pretend our business plan is realistic

I pretend people are honest with me

What Do *You* Pretend?

In the following list, mark each Pretend you are aware of doing. After you have completed the entire list, go back and mark the two you are aware of using most often.

I PRETEND . . .

I pretend to listen to people when I am not

I pretend to be interested when I am not

I pretend to agree

I pretend to care when I don't

I pretend to not care when I do

I pretend to not be as sensitive as I really am

I pretend to be tough

I pretend to not be judgmental

I pretend to not feel critical when I do

I pretend to know myself

I pretend to want to be self-aware

I pretend to want others to be open and honest with me

I pretend to be open

I pretend to not be defensive

I pretend to value openness

I pretend to want feedback about my competency

I pretend to want feedback about how it is to work with me

I pretend to want feedback from the people who report to me

I pretend to be honest

I pretend to trust people

I pretend to respect people that I don't

I pretend there is no us-and-them at work

I pretend to be supportive

I pretend to be enthusiastic when I don't feel it

I pretend to be optimistic when I am not

I pretend to be certain when I am not

I pretend to be patient

I pretend to like myself

I pretend to understand when I don't

I pretend to not be a perfectionist

I pretend to not understand when I do

I pretend to be stronger than I am

I pretend to not feel hurt when I do

I pretend to be more positive than I feel

I pretend to enjoy being with certain relatives

I pretend I feel secure

I pretend to not be depressed

I pretend to not feel afraid

I pretend to not feel sad when I do

I pretend to not feel angry when I am

I pretend being a single parent is not harder than it really is

I pretend to have family and work life in balance

I pretend to like where I live

I pretend to like my job

I pretend to be confident

I pretend to not worry about money

I pretend to feel better than I do

I pretend to not be competitive

I pretend lack of recognition doesn't bother me

I pretend to not care about people's opinions of me

I pretend to not feel as stressed as I do

I pretend to not care about myself

I pretend I don't drink too much

I pretend I take care of myself

I pretend to not be as worried about my children as I am

I pretend home life is going OK

I pretend I am not afraid for my parents' health

I pretend I do not feel lonely

I pretend to be happy

I pretend I don't blame others

I pretend to take responsibility for my life

I pretend I want to take responsibility for my life

I pretend I don't resent certain people

I pretend I don't have opinions that I do

I pretend to respect the company

I pretend our products and/or services are better than they are

I pretend to like my boss

I pretend to know what I am doing

I pretend I don't go along to get along

I pretend I am not in charge of my life

I pretend I am a victim

I pretend I am powerless

I pretend my life is under control

I pretend I like my life

If you completed the "I Pretend" inventory, assess how you are feeling:

Surprised? Smug? Irritated? Defensive? Exposed? Interested? Tired? Guilty?

What are you aware of having pretended all your life, even as a child?

How do you feel thinking about it? Justified? Smug? Irritated? Defensive? Somber? Self-critical? Guilty?

What percent of your daily life do you spend pretending?

Think of co-workers to whom you are currently pretending and what you are pretending. (Or, if you are a business consultant, clients.)

What are you afraid would happen if you were straight with them; that is, if you were open and real? What would you do if they asked what you are pretending with them?

Think of co-workers you sense are pretending with you, and what is being pretended. What are you afraid would happen if you told your co-workers what you think they are pretending?

If you were to add up all the pretending that goes on at the office in a given week, what percent of interactions would that be? How much time and energy are consumed needlessly?

Notice how automatically we pretend and how unaware of it we are, *or how unaware we want to be*. We pretend there is no pretending and that it doesn't matter. It's just business as usual. And so what? We're still in business.

How much does everyone just "live with it" or do "work-arounds"?

Or, perhaps this is simpler: When do you *not* pretend at the office?

Who sets the standards of openness and honesty in your team, department, company? If the boss sets the standard, what is the standard?

How well do your operational behaviors match the principles and company core values posted on the walls?

How do you know what is acceptable in your organization?

**Everything
that is going on
is acceptable.**

You are accepting it.

In *Winning,* Jack Welch notes that "[lack of candor] is a killer. Without candor, everyone saved face, and business lumbered along. The status quo was acceptable. Fake behavior was just a day at the office."

Fear as Usual is
Behavior as Usual is
Business as Usual

All trust issues

are really

fear issues.

Fear of what?

Disapproval

Being found out

Humiliation

Rejection

Being out, not in

Being ignored

Being a loser

Job loss

Failing at life

Being worthless

Being unworthy

Any or all of these seem to threaten survival.

Survival, Fear, and Deception

In 1912, "Yes-Man" first officially appeared in dictionaries, defined as "a person who agrees with everything that is said; *especially* one who endorses or supports without criticism every opinion or proposal of an associate or superior."

The Yes-Man strategy is "go along to get along," "don't rock the boat," and "tell 'em what they want to hear." All are survival strategies.

To what extent do you want those you manage to be afraid of you?

The prevailing management belief during the Industrial Revolution was that employees had to be afraid of their bosses or they would not work hard. While this is not as overt today, I find most employees are still afraid of their hierarchy.

If you have employees who report to you, consider the following:

- How afraid are they of you?
- How do you know this?
- If you don't know, how could you find out?
- How do you *benefit* from your employees *not* being open with you?

If they aren't open, honest, and real with you, yet you say you want them to be, you are either kidding yourself about that or unskilled at building trust with people. Either way, you are accountable for how it is. And how open, honest, and real are you being *with them?*

Employee references to "the pecking order" and "the food chain" within their organizations reveal anxiety and result in survival strategies in the form of defensive behaviors such as pretending, withholding, blaming, and Cover Your Ass (CYA), among many others. This anxiety surfaces in words and phrases such as:

- politically correct
- us-and-them
- scapegoat
- retaliation
- heads are going to roll
- cut off at the knees
- thrown under the bus
- hostile takeover
- victim of reductions-in-force or downsizings

In 2005, Art Wolfe, the world-renowned photographer, published *Vanishing Act—Camouflage as a Theme in Nature.* The following excerpts are from the introduction. (Words in parentheses are mine.)

> Deception, disguise, lures, and decoys appear to be the name of the game when it comes to species (employee) survival.
>
> For centuries, survival tactics amount to little more than a series of vanishing acts—the ability to confuse the eye of the predator or prey in an effort to simply

disappear. (Stay below the radar. Pretend. Withhold. Be a chameleon.)

Collectively, they illustrate the fierce evolutionary arms race between predator and prey (people), one that often rewards trickery, deception, and cryptic behavior as the winning strategies. (Witness office politics.)

And from David L. Smith's *Why We Lie: The Evolutionary Roots of Deception and the Unconscious Mind*:

> Even viruses . . . have subtle strategies for deceiving the immune systems of their hosts: nature is awash in deceit. Deceptive creatures have an edge over their competitors in the relentless struggle to survive and reproduce . . . As well-honed survival machines, human beings are also naturally deceptive. Deceit is . . . essential to our humanity but disowned by its perpetrators at every turn. Human society is a 'network of lies and deceptions'.
>
> The everyday game of strategic impression-management seethes with deception . . . Deception would appear to be the norm rather than the exception in business.

In a survey cited in James Patterson and Peter Kim's *The Day America Told the Truth*, when guaranteed anonymity, people admitted that they lied "regularly and often" at work.

Are you open and honest with your employees, co-workers, supervisors, and managers?

Therefore,
the
Usual
Agreement.

And yet, you say you hate being lied to . . .

and your own lying gnaws at you and won't go away in spite of your best efforts to justify, rationalize, and just forget about it.

So, now what?

Everything gets easier when we deal with our fear of one another.

"Courage is not the absence of fear, but rather the assessment that something else is more important."
–Franklin Delano Roosevelt

Ask yourself this:

1. Am I ready to stop being bullied by my own fear?
2. Am I going to stop withholding from all my co-workers?
3. Am I going to do what it takes to get co-workers to stop withholding from one another?
4. Am I going to do what it takes to get real, open, and honest feedback from coworkers about my competence, attitude, and trustworthiness (where "open" does not mean brutally honest, sugar-coated, or watered down)?

Only a heartfelt, courageous "Yes!" makes a New Agreement even possible. If your answer starts with "Yes, *but what about . . .*" or "Yes, *but how do you . . .*" stop right there. You're already hedging. Any form of "Yes but . . ." always means "No." All "how-to's" are really a search to figure out how to be open and still have everyone remain comfortable (aka: still like you).

Do you want to be comfortable or be real? Pick one.

This is a one-day-at-a-time deal, like deciding to become physically fit. Every day, be more open than you used to be. While recovering from a lifetime of pretending, you will struggle to resist the incessant, seductive pull of your comfort zone. Your commitment covers one sentence at a time, one interaction at a time, one day at a time. The New Agreement is an ongoing recovery process. Don't allow yourself to be stymied by trying to do this perfectly. Just jump in.

"Freedom's just another word for nothing left to hide."
–Susan Campbell,
Getting Real

"Real problems
get solved
when the people
solving them
get real."
–Don White

PART II

THE NEW AGREEMENT

The New Agreement

***Accountability* is the New Agreement. Accountability requires Self-Awareness, Openness, *and* Courage.**

Accountability

Complete accountability means I take 100% responsibility for my awareness, attitude, behavior (especially defensiveness), and experience—always and everywhere. I don't blame others, myself, or circumstances. I notice and own my choices and the consequences of those choices. Accountability is about cause and effect, not good/bad/right/wrong. Accountability is *not* blame.

Self-Awareness

I am open to knowing myself: my thoughts, feelings, and attitude. I am aware of my defenses and the fears producing them. I seek and welcome feedback to prevent self-deception. I am aware of the effect my personal issues have in the workplace.

Openness

I do not withhold. I am spontaneous. I say what I am thinking, feeling, sensing, and wondering. I ask straight questions. I give straight, complete answers. I ask for what I want. I know where I stand with all my co-workers, including supervisors and managers, regarding their total experience of working and dealing with me.

You can be honest without being open, but you cannot be open without also being honest. "I will not be open with you" is honest but not open, by declaration. *"Brutally honest" is unaccountable.*

Daily practice of the New Agreement transforms you and your organization.

At first, being real feels uncomfortable and vulnerable to disapproval, criticism, judgments, and manipulation.

Later, *not* being real feels intolerable.

"We're not communicating" is never true. Anytime you are anywhere near another human being you are communicating.

Anything that involves me having an experience of you and you having an experience of me constitutes communication.

In *every* interaction with another person you are training that person how to treat you.

It is useful to realize that you own every aspect of every relationship you are in. This does *not* mean you are responsible for the other person in the relationship.

Anytime you have two people working to- gether, you will have issues. You can either bury them or work them out, cover them up or clear them up.

Trust-building is about facing and dealing with real issues.

A "real" issue is any issue that causes high levels of anxiety just *thinking* about it.

Without trust, you cannot have a committed work force. Mistrust precludes it.

Conversations and meetings go in circles because we do not want to be straight with one another. It's not about IQ or comprehension. Indirectness is a collusion. You cannot be indirect with me without my allowing it.

Defensive behaviors, such as blaming and pretending, are noxious and the source of almost all trouble between people.

What's the use of "open door" policies if the people behind the desks are defensive and their *internal* doors are closed?

As an annual line item, what do you think the collective defensiveness of your workforce is costing the business?

How would you even know?

We do not consider employee morale as a factor in the financial state of our businesses, but in fact, it is a major factor. About improvements of statistical controls in business, W. Edwards Deming, acclaimed creator of The Deming Method of modern management, said, "The most important numbers in business are unknown and unknowable. For example, what is the cost of employee morale? The economic losses from fear are appalling. Where there is fear, there will be wrong figures."

Defensiveness is a business cost, *not* a cost of doing business.

Defensiveness

You are accountable for your defensiveness.

No one can make you defensive. Becoming defensive is a choice.

The Source of Defensiveness

As human beings, we are hardwired from very early in our evolution to react instantly to perceived physical threats. It so happens that psychological threats have the same effect: they instantly trigger all our survival alarms. Even though your survival is not physically threatened, your Image Management Department, home of your unconscious (unaware) insecurities left over from childhood, reacts defensively to one or all of the following fears from daily events and interactions with people:

You fear:

1. You will be thought of as insignificant and then ignored; incompetent and then humiliated; unlikable and then disliked.
2. You will appear to be insignificant and then ignored; incompetent and then humiliated, unlikable and then disliked.
3. You *are* insignificant; incompetent, and unlikeable/ unlovable.
4. You are powerless to change any of the above.

The less aware you are of the above fears when they happen, the more defensive you will be.

Essential to being defensive less often is to be aware more often.

Signs of Defensiveness

The following is a list of common defenses we use rather than being self-aware and accountable. The list is not an assessment. Its purpose is to deepen your awareness and understanding. I get defensive daily. My goal is to notice it right away and replace it with accountability. Because of what happened to us and around us during our most formative years, we get defensive easily.

Mark all the ones that you are aware of using. After you have completed the list, go back through and mark the two that you use most often. If after completing the list you have not marked any, explore **Denying** and **Pretending**.

- ☒ Loss of humor
- ☒ Trivializing with humor (laughing it off)
- ☒ A high charge or energy in the body (feeling flush, shallow breathing, tight throat)
- ☐ Sudden drop in I.Q. ("I don't know; I'm so confused.")
- ☐ *Having* to be right all the time (versus *wanting* to be right)
- ☐ Wanting the last word (frequently with rise in volume of voice)
- ☒ Flooding others with information to prove a point
- ☒ Endless explaining, rationalizing or justifying (It's important to know the difference between explaining and justifying. Explaining is descriptive. Justifying is

proving, and is unaccountable and defensive because it is intended to preempt resistance.)

- ☒ Playing "poor me"
- ☒ Teaching, preaching, or speech-making
- ☒ Blaming
- ☐ Denying
- ☐ Pretending
- ☒ Being too nice (frequently used by "people pleasers")
- ☒ Poker face (masks)
- ☒ Sarcasm or cynicism
- ☐ Illness
- ☒ Withdrawal into deadly silence; avoiding
- ☐ The typology excuse ("That's my personality/style," or "That's just how I am.")
- ☐ Terminal uniqueness ("I'm different from everyone else. You won't figure me out.")
- ☐ Rigidity
- ☐ Intellectualizing
- ☐ Criticizing; shaming
- ☐ Anger; attack (the best defense is a good offense)
- ☒ Holding a grudge
- ☐ Indignation (taking offense)
- ☐ Enlightened ("I'm aware of that, leave me alone")
- ☐ Selective deafness (hearing only what you want to hear)
- ☐ Suddenly tired or sleepy
- ☐ Addictions (foods, work, television, shopping, drugs, gambling)
- ☐ Caretaking; rescuing
- ☐ Harried; too busy to _____
- ☐ Emotionalism*

* This list is reprinted with permission: © 2018 Business Consultants, Inc.

Considering the above list, notice how *common* defensive behaviors are.

What percent of your daily life do you spend being defensive? Or look at it this way: When are you *not* defensive? Either way, how do you know?

Think about giving the list of Signs of Defensiveness to several co-workers and to your boss, asking them to mark which defenses they notice you do.

How do you think they would react?

How awkward would you feel?

Think they would be honest?

Which ones do you think they would mark about you?

If you got a Usual Agreement response, what would you do, given a commitment to the New Agreement?

Here are some usual rationalizations for defensive behaviors:

- He/She/It made me defensive
- It's just another day at the office
- It's just how people are
- Everybody does it
- Just "live with it"
- Do "workarounds"
- It's just how it is around here
- It's just business as usual
- It's no big deal
- It really doesn't matter anyway

The 1% Rule — Don't Leave Home without It

Your fear triggers defensiveness instantly, without your being conscious of it at first. However, using the 1% Rule will immediately begin to activate the antidote: self-awareness and accountable choices. This essential technique is regarded as invaluable by those practicing ACT.

It works like this: as soon as you notice you are experiencing signs of defensiveness, ask yourself, "What *is* true about this feedback?"

If you earnestly search for what *is* true about the feedback, you *will* find at least 1% that is true, for starters. To take back more conscious control of yourself, notice what fears you are experiencing in the moment. Ask yourself what you're afraid the feedback or interaction says or does not say about you and about how you want to be perceived. For example:

"Seems to me that you are being defensive right now."

"Really? I don't like hearing that. Tell me what you're seeing. I want to be aware of it so I can deal with it right now."

This receptivity stops denial, generates constructive self-control, and creates connection with the person giving you the feedback, rather than rejection. This self-inquiry *must be heartfelt* or you are not truly open to being aware and accountable at that moment, rather than remaining defensive.

The more you
resist feedback,
the more you're
afraid it's really true.
If you do not feel
threatened,
you do not get
defensive. Period.

Defensiveness Is Unaccountable

Denial — The Most Insidious Defense of All

Denial completely precludes any accountability, blocking any possibility of problem-solving and resolution.

For example:

> "Seems to me that you are being defensive right now."

> "No, I'm not."

> "Seems to me you have to be right about everything your team does."

> "No, I don't."

Racism, Sexism, and the 1% rule

The 1% Rule is the only way to combat racism and sexism. Born in 1944 and raised in the American South, I ingested racism and sexism osmotically. During college in the 1960s in Memphis, Tennessee, I became aware of this programming. Painfully aware. In spite of "knowing better" and the obvious toxicity of both racism and sexism, they were deeply embedded in my unconscious. Being accountable for all my interactions, I frequently ask others for feedback about this blind spot.

Always assume you *are* some way that you *really* don't want to be (for example: some traits of your mother or father), rather than assuming you are not that way.

Liar Liar — Jim Carrey

Disclosures that are commonly referred to as "too honest" suggest they are problematic. Typically, they amount to *brutal* honesty, and reveal previously denied or withheld negativity by the speaker.

In the 1997 movie *Liar Liar*, Jim Carrey plays a lawyer who wreaks havoc when placed under a spell condemning him to be truthful for twenty-four chaotic and agonizing hours. The movie illustrated the common belief that if one is "completely" honest it will be nothing but trouble. But most of what the lawyer blurted out was *brutal* honesty and *unaccountable*. It amounted to criticism of some sort or another. Given that, of course his interactions were trouble. The turning point in the movie happened when his awareness of his own role in the mess he had made of his life—especially with his young son—dawned on him. With this realization, he took responsibility for his previous choices, actions, and troubles, which was (and is) humbling and restorative.

It is *un*accountable openness that has given openness a bad name. I suspect it is because of unaccountable openness that the old adage "If you can't say something nice, don't say anything" emerged.

The following are commonly considered honesty but they are not accountable:

Being Brutally Honest

How do you feel when someone says he or she is going to be "brutally honest" with you? You probably brace for some kind of negative dump.

Brutally honest is about brutality, *not* about honesty.
Being "brutally honest" is an excuse and an attempt to legitimize being critical of someone. It usually is preceded by some sort of disclaimer for any responsibility for how it lands on the other person, like, "Well, if you want me to be brutally honest . . ." or "Well, to be brutally honest . . ." It's another form of a cheap shot, as are criticizing and blaming.

Then, when the recipient gets upset, the other person throws up his hands to indicate his innocence, saying, "I'm just being honest (like you wanted) . . ."

Honest, yes. Accountable, no. It's a cheap shot.

How about the times *you* are brutally honest (which you learned to do early in your life just as everyone else did)? Notice that when you label your comments "brutally honest" they amount to criticisms, and usually are an upset that you have been withholding.

Criticizing Others
How do you like being criticized?

Almost everyone reacts defensively, feels offended, and rebuts the criticism in some way, including a counterattack. The interaction is negative, dissatisfying, and erodes trust. And, depending upon the tone of the interaction, results in resentment, retaliation, and grudges. Name-calling—such as, "You are a jerk; jackass; loser; wimp; slug; screw-up; chicken-shit," etc., including racial slurs—is just another form of criticism.

Critical adults were strongly criticized as children.

Learn to distinguish between sharing an observation, however strongly felt, and being critical or judgmental.

Blaming and Shaming Others

Looking for a fight? Blame somebody, anybody.

As a child, you didn't look forward to being blamed and shamed. As an adult, you still don't like it. (And your kids don't like it any more than you do!)

Blaming and shaming are counterproductive.

Almost anyone becomes instantly defensive, negating the accusation and counterattacking. Now the battle is on. Blaming is all about *assigning fault.* Who welcomes that? "Cover Your Ass" is the common strategy in the workplace to pre-empt or deal with blame attacks. If you want to get a negative reaction from someone, blame them, including using "loaded questions" (see Part III, p. 109).

The Ain't It Awful Club

People who do not want to take responsibility for their lives inhabit the role and realm of Victimhood. I've yet to begin work with a company in which there wasn't an "Ain't It Awful Club" established somewhere therein. This is the group of employees who are negative, cynical, and incessant critics and complainers about everything and everybody else in the company. They find one another like magnets and form a support group for The Unaccountable. They are the consummate victims of the employee body, absolving themselves of any responsibility for their experience while loudly assigning their plight to being the fault of others. They are wholesale blamers. Who in your organization comes to mind?

Shaming

"We don't yet know, above all, what the world might be like if children were to grow up without being subjected to humiliation; if parents would respect them and talk to them seriously as people (equals)."—Alice Miller

The threat of shaming and humiliating one another to control and manipulate behavior is as old as humanity and worldwide. Religions institutionalized its use. Even children wield this toxic venom on one another, having learned it well at home. "Losing face" is regarded as the most horrific experience of all in Asian cultures, and the way many Asians live their lives is dominated by this fear.

Literary references to being a "laughingstock" appeared as early as the 1500s.

The *tone* of shaming is especially caustic. It is derisive and condemning. There is an implied "you should be ashamed of yourself!" in the tone, which adds salt to the wound. *It is a form of bullying.* Having originated in our childhoods, being shamed elicits very strong reactions, including resentment. Shaming has a long half-life.

Blaming attacks what you did or did not do. Shaming goes beyond the behavior focus and is meant to attack your very core. It attacks your identity, *who you are* as a person, your worth. Shaming is *meant* to be demeaning and taken personally. It is vindictive. It condemns your character. Shaming feels so devastating to most people that consciously or unconsciously we maintain a lifelong, daily vigil to avoid at all costs finding ourselves "On the Spot" and subsequently "dying of embarrassment." Why do we associate "death" with this experience, as in "*dying* of embarrassment"?

The elaborate extent to which organizations will go, especially within the hierarchy, to avoid embarrassment implies the power of this frightful prospect. Witness the widespread support for *anonymous* feedback, which is then reviewed with the recipient in private.

aversion to "feeling vulnerable" stems from our fear of humiliation or being taken advantage of.

Become a Recovering Blamer

To become accountable *requires* you to continually reduce your inclination to blame others. I frequently compare it to deciding to end an addiction. Given that our social norm is to be unaccountable, you will be surrounded by people who are still playing the "Blame 'n' Shame Game." Therefore, *not* to blame will take great personal strength and discipline. Blaming and shaming are seductive defense mechanisms powered by intense insecurities and fear. Blaming offers an escape from taking 100% responsibility for yourself and your experience. Self-criticism and self-blame are equally toxic and formidable to overcome. Often pathological, they are devastating to your vital sense of self-worth. To replace blaming and shaming with compassion is perhaps the most life-giving thing you can do for yourself and your relationship with others. Undertaking this is a life-long practice.

If blaming and shaming were removed from an organization, everyone there would become more transparent and accountable.

When you are less defensive you are more transparent and more prone to be trusted. Others naturally enjoy being around you and are inclined to be receptive, open, friendly, helpful, and cooperative toward you. You are experienced as approachable and "user friendly" rather than contentious, suspicious, and guarded. Being conscientious about not becoming defensive in conversations and interactions at work results in satisfying, productive, trusting relationships.

"Through being transparent, you learn that you are most lovable when you are most transparent—that people want to love you if you will just let yourself be seen."

–Susan Campbell,
Getting Real

The New Agreement is a recovery model, *not* a perfection model. Continuously improving your application of ACT means you are less defensive more often and clean up and clear up issues with co-workers when they happen rather than delaying.

Accountable
Openness
is what happens
when you stop
being defensive.

Accountable Openness

How to Free Yourself from Defensiveness

Become Enlightened.

Until then, here's the deal:

The extent to which you fear and believe you are insignificant, incompetent, and unlikable has built up over your lifetime. Because you don't like feeling these insecurities, you "hide" them in your unconscious. If you knew how to rid yourself of them, you would have done it by now rather than manage them with denial and other energy-draining defense mechanisms. Meanwhile, they remain the source of your defensiveness.

Because you construct your defenses, you can choose to deactivate them.

Remember, no one can *make you* defensive, but until you choose to awaken your self-awareness, it *does* seem like other people are causing you to become defensive. Because it is a survival mechanism, this happens unconsciously and instantaneously. Suddenly you are defensive. Looking back, you think, "What happened? One minute I was fine and then 'boom!' I was all worked up and out of control."

Choosing self-awareness, followed by self-disclosure, frees you from descending into the morass of defensiveness.

Self-Awareness to the Rescue

You *must own* that you *are* afraid (like everyone else) of being insignificant, incompetent, and unlikable, which is evidenced by the simple fact of your getting defensive. Never mind arguing to what degree it's true. That's just your Image Management Department attempting damage control. Let it go.

Decide to meet your fears with openness in the moment. *Before* the fear gets diverted to your unconscious by your Image Management Department and then manifests as defensive behavior, tell yourself that now you *want* to be aware of the slightest hint of feeling any one of the following fears:

- Ignored and not as included as you want to be at the moment
- Humiliated and not being seen or thought of as competent in some way
- Disliked by a coworker or group that matters to you

The more you understand the ways we all are dealing with fear, the less judgmental and the more compassionate you become.

Commit to raising, rather than dulling, your sensitivity to these insecurities. Have the interest of a scientist doing research, always being on the lookout for them. Be vigilant. Detect their earliest onset. In this way, our fears about ourselves become interesting and manageable, rather than causing defensiveness problems. As Susan Campbell notes in *Getting Real*:

> You can only be as authentic as you are self-aware. The first most important part of being transparent is seeing yourself without praise or blame. Seeing yourself is an act of observation, not of evaluation.

How to Start Difficult Conversations

I include this information because ever since 1990, ACT workshop attendees tell Don and me how effective and valuable the approach described below has proven to be for them.

When you are anticipating having an awkward or difficult conversation, the way to get past being stuck about what to say, or being reluctant to say it, is to start the conversation by talking about your own fear of having it. Express your feelings of uncertainty, awkwardness, and anxiety before getting into the issue itself. Talk about *yourself* first, before bringing in your experience of the other person/people.

Expressing your **first fear first**, in a straightforward manner, will curtail your tendency to start off with blame or criticism.

Lead with your **first fear first**, such as:

- "I'm afraid talking about this will just make things worse and jeopardize our friendship."
- "I'm afraid what I want to say isn't important to you and you won't want to hear it."
- "I'm scared I made a poor decision here and that you'll be angry when I tell you about it, and I always want to avoid conflict."
- "I'm not sure of my thinking on this topic and I'm reluctant to share it with you for fear of looking stupid."
- "As a new hire, I'm afraid to offer my suggestions about how certain procedures are carried out in the department."
- "I'm afraid not having a college degree limits my credibility."

In these examples, the speaker is being open about him/herself in the moment. This kind of non-defensive self-disclosure—

especially if said cleanly, without drama—usually generates receptivity, because it certainly is not an aggressive start or tone. It is not the typical opening remark that would come from a person ready to do battle. Also, it gives the listener guidance for where to start the conversation because the speaker has openly identified his/her immediate concern(s) about the relationship itself, and that he/she cares about it. Non-defensiveness is a relaxed, receptive posture and tone.

The Practice of Self-Awareness Plus Self-Disclosure

Upon becoming aware of a fear, treat it with interest, like an investigator, rather than with alarm. Describe it something like this:

> Ha. Look at this. I notice I'm feeling afraid that I might be mistaken about our sales projections for next quarter. I'm also afraid the boss is going to be angry if the numbers are off and he'll begin to think I'm not capable of handling the forecasts. I want to know if any of this is true. I'm going to go ask him right now, and also find out how he sees my performance in this new role. I will get perfectly clear about where I stand in his eyes before I leave the meeting. I want to know today if he has concerns about my competence. I don't want to kid myself, and I don't want him to kid me, either.

The New Agreement embraces *complete* accountability. No hiding. No waiting for the "appropriate" time (which never arrives). *Consciously* acknowledge the fear before it gets traction, lest you end up being defensive.

However, when fears *do* go unnoticed and show defensiveness (which will happen daily), you treat th of awareness with the light of openness, too. Imagine you are in a project review meeting with your team. Accountability would be to declare out loud what you are noticing. Something like:

> I've interrupted you twice and was about to do it again but just became aware that I am feeling defensive and I'm not listening to you. I've been criticizing you silently and thinking how to show you're wrong and I'm right about the project status. I want to avoid responsibility for any breakdowns because I might look incompetent to all of you and confirm a fear that I have about being over my head in this new role. My Image Management Department is trying to strangle me right now. So, I would like to hear from each of you about how well you think I am working out in this role and as a team member. Straight up and direct, please. No sugar coating or watering down.

Thus, The New Agreement.

"Yeah, but that would take too long and take up meeting time," you say.

Nope.

Accountable people are direct and immediate in their communication. *They own whatever is going on in the meeting.* Everyone in the meeting is a smoke detector. It's a business meeting, after all, and the meeting is everybody's business, unlike business-as-usual, wherein the one person in charge of the meeting or even some designated facilitator is expected to handle the group dynamics and make the meeting worthwhile (the parent-child or teacher-student relationship).

To maintain transformation and trust, they *know* how vital it is to deal with fear immediately, anytime, anywhere. Fear is *the* show-stopper. "Scared stiff" means just what it implies. This is as true for organizations as it is for individuals and for the human body. It is a direct hit to efficiency, effectiveness, and the bottom line. (For more on this, see pp. 122ff.)

You will be astonished at how lean and complete feedback exchanges become among employees applying The New Agreement.

**Gamechanger:
Being Accountably Open in the following ways:**

1. Become aware of what *you* did (or did not do) to contribute to the situation or issue
2. Be open about this awareness
3. Be open about *not* wanting to take responsibility for your part
4. Be open about wanting to blame other people and say who they are
5. Be open about whatever fear(s) you are having about all this as it relates to your significance, competence, or likeability
6. Be open about *not* wanting to be open *about any of this*
7. Insist on everyone else being accountably open

The plethora of studies and books defending lying and withholding do not acknowledge or even consider this powerful combination of self-awareness and self-disclosure, **but in forty years of work I have never seen accountable openness fail to resolve an interpersonal issue and engender trust in the process.**

Your commitment to practice accountable openness one sentence at a time, one conversation at a time, one person at a time, one day at a time will build and strengthen your self-respect, presence, effectiveness, and trustworthiness.

Actually *being* accountably open is not as scary as thinking about doing it. Best to "just do it."

Seeking and Embracing Feedback

Make It "Safe"

You cannot mandate openness. You cannot command a workforce not to be afraid, to just be open and trust one another. That approach creates its opposite.

You *can*, however, invite and *inspire* openness by being the most open when it is the most difficult.

No motivational speech or moralizing sermon will convert a workforce to openness. If so, everyone who heard it would be moved to action, but they are not. Speeches can invite and *inspire* a listener to take action, but not *cause* action.

The difference between those who take action and those who do not is a result of *a decision to be real*, regardless of the consequences.

Safety is an illusion.

All our talk about creating a "safe" environment for openness within part or all of an organization simply legitimizes and institutionalizes closed-ness. *Anonymous* feedback formulas, the bread and butter of traditional Organizational Development specialists, only reflect and feed our fear of openness. The same goes for the contrived "sandwiching" formulas. What could be more appealing than a consultant who assures the client that they can "build trust" while avoiding awkward, "uncomfortable" employee interactions at the same time? That's just what the buyer wants to hear. The consultant gets to stay comfortable as well, professing that "everybody knows" it's too dangerous for people to give feedback face-to-face, and especially to their boss.

I have forty years of experience to the contrary.

So, never mind about creating a "safe" environment for openness. Just be one of these: someone in your organization who is the first to be open and accountable. Then you are the leader, no matter your rank or title. Be someone to follow.

> # The more often you choose the *courage* to be accountable, the more you—and not your fear—control your life and inspire those around you to do the same. Are you up for that?

"Job Security"

If there is anything akin to "security" on the job, it would amount to knowing exactly how you and your work are perceived by everyone you deal with. If you're not up to snuff technically or interpersonally, *it's best to know it immediately* so you can do something about it, rather than waiting until your boss has found your replacement.

Your boss doesn't fire you, he just brings you the news. The people who work with and around you fire you in a business-as-usual workplace.

In an accountable culture, *you* are responsible for knowing how your technical competence is perceived by those who work with you, as well as how they experience you interpersonally. (This is ongoing and in addition to any semi-annual-type performance reviews with your manager.) In getting feedback, it is your responsibility to do what it takes to get whomever you are talking with to be honest, open, and complete with you (about anything). It is not acceptable or accountable to claim "no one told me" or "no one will tell me."

The New Agreement means: I can find out how you think and feel about me, my work, and how it is to work with me anytime I want to know. From there we work things out.

No one can withhold from you without you allowing it. Being bullshitted is a collusion.

"What do you like/not like about me?"

What do you think would happen if you ask co-workers what they like and do not like about you? (This is a different question from "Do you like me?")

Notice how you feel contemplating such interactions. How willing are you to try this? What are you afraid might happen when you ask for this from coworkers? Whose response would you trust? If you didn't trust a response, what would you do? If you think you trust someone, how do you explain your reluctance to ask for this information from him or her? What agreement runs the relationship?

Openness gets complicated only when you don't want to do it.

Being real with others is your best bet for being trusted and respected, though not necessarily liked. Being liked is different from being trusted and respected. Some people will not like you no matter what you say or do, usually because they feel afraid in some way. Like racists, for example, if you are the object of their judgments.

"People pleasers," addicted to being liked and therefore adverse to confrontation and uncomfortable interactions, struggle with the openness part of accountability. They support the "let's not go there" camp when it comes to "uncomfortable" feedback. They want only "positive" or "constructive" feedback exchanges. With ACT, the only "negative" feedback is that which you tell someone else about me rather than say it to me directly. Telling someone else indicates you do not respect me enough to be straight up with me and are "bad mouthing" me behind my back. (For more on this, see "Triangulation," page 120).

From the ACT point of view, feedback is neither positive nor negative. It can be accountable or unaccountable. Some of it you will like and some you will not like. Although accountable feedback is always far more effective and useful, to get unaccountable feedback is better than none at all because at least you know more about where you stand with someone.

"But what about abusive feedback?" you might ask.

Confront it.

What you experience as abusive, manipulative, or malicious feedback *lasts exactly as long as you let it. You get what you put up with.* What feels abusive to you may not feel the same to someone else. It is useful to learn why the coworker feels as they do and to determine what, if anything, you can do about it, entrenched bias, prejudices and stereotypes notwithstanding.

The Spot — The Place Where You Die of Embarrassment

In business-as-usual cultures everyone avoids being put on the spot by subscribing to The Usual Agreement. The deal is "I won't put you on the spot and you don't put me on the spot." This collusion to maintain The Comfort Zone stops feedback cold. Like the relationship between junkies and dealers, each depends on the other to keep the dysfunction going. Alcoholics hang around with other alcoholics to insulate themselves from reality and to avoid taking responsibility for their actions and their lives. The same phenomenon shows up in business organizations committed to non-confrontational, polite avoidance of any direct, open, and real communication. Welcome, anonymous feedback advocates.

Are you aware of how afraid you are of dying of embarrassment, and how it runs your life?

By stark contrast, consider the intensely performance-driven endeavors of Olympians. Everything they do is continually videoed by their coaching staff so the performer can have the most comprehensive feedback possible. It is imperative to world-class endeavors. Imagine the effect on an athlete's, artist's or medical student's development if they were given only feedback deemed comfortable.

Openness Lite

In business organizations, I call the common practice of sugarcoating and watering down feedback (and any other information) "Openness Lite." This includes any form of "360" feedback that is anything other than face-to-face, *especially* anything that is anonymous. The belief seems to be that the hapless employees will become traumatized by hearing one another's impressions, opinions, thoughts, and feelings about them, their work, and how it is to work with one another. The implication seems to be they are too dim-witted, fragile, or mean-spirited to do so. Heaven forbid that employees would tell their boss how they *really* feel about them! Openness Lite reflects the lack of competence on the part of management to understand accountability and to deal with defensiveness. A costly limitation.

"The opposite of polite is not rude. The opposite of polite is real. The effectiveness of a team is inversely proportional to its politeness." –Don White

Employees are not only perfectly capable of giving and receiving feedback in person, they thrive on it. I have never seen otherwise. It is managers and supervisors who resist it because, lacking competency in dealing with interpersonal and group dynamics, they fear losing control.

The New Agreement handles the fear-based "Openness Lite." Instead of taking feedback off-line as if shameful or devastating, face-to-face feedback happens spontaneously, grown-up to grown-up, anytime, anywhere. Avoiding this is disrespectful and disempowering.

"It's time to stop acting mortally wounded when someone says he doesn't like something we did. It's time to give one another credit for being able to handle honest feedback. Let's put more value on seeing what is than on being comfortable."
–Susan Campbell, *Getting Real*

I Think You're Kidding Yourself
"Self-deception is any mental process or behavior the function of which is to conceal information from one's own conscious mind."
–David L Smith, *Why We Lie*

Self-deception is like a drug induced to avoid some aspect of your reality.

It's useful to assume that you are always kidding yourself about something at work (if not in your life altogether). Staying real with your self-perception *requires* feedback. Feedback is the *only* way to avoid self-deception and denial, which are the very opposite of being accountable and non-defensive.

Real friends don't let friends kid themselves.
Straight feedback keeps relationships straight.

An *essential component* of self-awareness and effectiveness is to know your coworkers' experience of you. They can see you more accurately than you can see yourself at times, especially when your Image Management Department is running the show. *Your* commitment to The New Agreement will be tested when you don't like what you are hearing. *Their* commitment to The New Agreement will be tested when they fear you will not like what they have to say and will dislike them for saying it.

Get Over Being Offended

Feeling offended is always a choice.

Taking offense at feedback that we feel threatened by is a defensive response common to all of us. We even frequently attempt to preempt this response by saying "Don't take it personally," which practically guarantees the recipient *will* take it personally.

Through practice you can reprogram yourself to avoid reacting defensively. You can hear the feedback to be about what you are doing (or not doing), *rather* than about who you are as a human being.

"Eliminate the phrase 'don't take it personally' from your vocabulary—it's insulting."–Kim Scott, *Radical Candor*

When you're not being defensive, you will find others' opinions of you interesting or even useful, but not offensive or threatening. Receptivity replaces resistance and defensiveness. Problem-solving (if there is a problem) happens. Negativity and breakdowns do not occur.

Support for Getting Real

I know of no one who has successfully managed to deal with their defensiveness on their own.

You and I *must* be part of a recovery group, and the workplace is perhaps the best place for it. At work, you are interacting daily and frequently with a team, department, or group of colleagues. Opportunities to have ongoing, in-the-moment feedback abound. Receiving feedback *is essential* to self-awareness, accountability, and quick recovery from self-deception. When you and your co-workers are as committed to The New Agreement as you are to all other business goals, the transformative power of Accountable Communication will flourish, building solid trust in the process.

"Your honest feedback or response is the greatest gift you can give to another person."
–Susan Campbell, *Getting Real*

The Stop-Start-Continue Feedback Process

One of the most effective means of making Accountable Communication Technology (ACT) part of a company's culture is the practice of a feedback process called Stop-Start-Continue (SSC).

Don White, co-founding partner of Barton White Associates, began using SSC systematically in the late 1980s during his tenure at Procter & Gamble. When he first began using SSC with the hourly workforce on the factory floor, a grievance was filed immediately. Two years later, after he had been using SSC there regularly as a formal feedback process, he was visiting another facility and the regularly scheduled session at his facility was not held. That generated a grievance, too. This was the one and only time Don had the experience of a grievance reversal in his twenty-seven years at Procter & Gamble. The workforce had come to value SSC sessions as the best way to influence their co-workers and have control of their daily work life.

We introduce SSC to organizations we work with to support their practice of The New Agreement. The following is an overview of the process and is not intended to be instructions for how to hold or facilitate an SSC session. We facilitate several of a team's or group's early SSC sessions, and then train managers how to facilitate the sessions.

Depending upon team size, each member will be the designated recipient of the group feedback session at least twice a year. For the very first session, we have the supervisor or manager be the first person to receive everyone's feedback. Among other things, this gives us a clear sense of how afraid the team members are of their boss.

Notice your response as you imagine this happening in your organization.

The session begins immediately with everyone, including the designated recipient, filling out a sheet that has the words "Stop," "Start," and "Continue" equally spaced down the left margin of an otherwise blank page.

For ten minutes (in silence) each person writes down what he or she wants the recipient to stop doing, start doing, and continue doing. ("Stops" might be "I want you to stop coming to meetings late," or "Stop pretending to listen to me when I am talking with you," or "Stop agreeing when you don't," or "Stop complaining about people," etc.) Next, each person states out loud one "Stop" when it is their turn until all "Stops" have been spoken. Unless the recipient is unclear about a request, there is *no* discussion about the content of any SSC. This is not a problem-solving session. If the recipient doesn't like what is said, his or her job is to notice their defensiveness silently, use the 1% Rule, and take it up with the person *after* the SSC session.

A note about "fair" feedback

There is no such thing as "fair" or "valid" feedback. *All feedback is an opinion*, and opinions are a collage of co-workers' experiences of one another. Feedback is never The Truth. Relationships are the sum of ongoing opinions of one another. For that reason, others' opinions of you are the operative context for your interactions and work together. The *only* value of the content of any feedback (as well as the tone with which it is delivered) is its *utility* to you.

Among skills required for an effective SSC session, listening non-defensively is certainly one. "Starts" could include "Start speaking up in meetings," or "Start taking breaks during the day," or "Start taking the Quality initiative seriously," or "Start looking at me when you are talking to me," or "Start showing up like you want to be on this team." As with Stops, each person states aloud one Start until all have been read.

"Continues" could include "Continue being conscientious," or "Continue being patient with me until I get better at our new IT system," or "Continue to work on being less defensive."

After the "Continue" rounds are complete, everyone passes their sheets with their SSCs written on them to the recipient. The recipient then has a record of all the feedback. No one else has a copy. The recipient will ingest it all and decide what to do with it, if anything. Follow-up conversations usually happen right away. This will not be the last SSC session the recipient will have with the team and the manager. Knowing that, recipients are wise to make changes in attitudes, behaviors, and the quality of relationships.

As well as having teammates included in the SSC session, recipients are urged to invite any other coworkers with whom they interface and want SSC feedback from. The quality and value of any SSC session is dependent upon the honesty and accountability of all participants. No feedback form or structure of any kind can force this critical factor. In an accountable organization, SSC sessions are viewed to be as important as other business meetings. Participation is no more optional than it is for a product quality review meeting.

Think about how an SSC session would go with your team. Would there be resistance or receptivity? Would it be tense or relaxed? Would the group be cautious and superficial, or authentic?

Most employees become very anxious when the SSC session is described to them because of their fear of feedback in public. This is an important opportunity for their designated leaders to lead—by going first. Sooner than later, his or her vulnerability is appreciated by the others present, bringing everyone's humanness to the surface. Courage is infectious. As each member's "Stops" become less superficial and more real, the fear of humiliation decreases. They are breaking down the traditional walls between boss and reports. It is the beginning of a different sense of connection, which grows ever stronger as the SSC sessions evolve over time from "unnatural" to natural. Getting real gets easier, but more importantly—it gets appealing.

Start-Stop-Continue at Medical Eye Center

The following is a review of SSC by the Clinical Director of Medical Eye Center in Medford, Oregon:

> We have been using SSC at Medical Eye Center for almost twenty years. Employees fondly refer to these sessions as 'flossing'. I have witnessed a distinct difference between teams that use SSC regularly and those that do not. Given the intense demands of a medical services practice, without regular 'interpersonal hygiene', painful decay in the quality of relationships inevitably happens.
>
> I was first introduced to this process while in charge of our LASIK surgery team. This team was made up of 'A' team players, meaning those who had strong personalities and wanted to be seen as stars. It was not unusual to have conflict on the team due to their competitive dynamic. Soon after the SSC process was introduced, we saw a definite decrease in the amount

of conflict. The expectation was now in place that team members would continually share feedback with one another. The early sessions released the tension that had built up over time. Everyone reported that being open felt much better than withholding from one another. Fear was no longer determining their interactions. Soon they were giving feedback in the moment and not waiting for the next SSC session. Over time, the process became much faster because superficial feedback stopped and more substantial, useful, and specific feedback became the norm. They had taken ownership of the quality of their relationships and their SSC sessions.

We use the SSC process to address issues on any team. In another case, one of the teams in our oculoplastic department had developed noticeable tension and drama with one another, although they claimed to be 'tight knit' and 'just like family'.

When I scheduled them for a series of SSC sessions, they protested that it would 'damage' their relationships, but the truth was they feared the sessions might reveal the withholding and triangulating that was pervasive in the group.

I facilitated their SSC sessions. Predictably, the issues did surface. While SSC sessions reveal the status of work relationships and work problems, the sessions are never punitive. The format naturally sets solutions in motion. Their first session was long, but they began to get real with one another, and the relief was palatable. Every few weeks I facilitated another session for them until each team member had been the 'focal' person for a session. I always feel both compassion and pride as I witness the re-building of healthy, accountable relationships. Like other groups, they simply had not known how to break out of their spiral of pretending and superficial friendships.

Recently we added several new physicians to the practice. Each physician has a team made up of newer staff. With any new team there are a host of challenges that take place before the members finds their rhythm and coordination. Our new physicians have implemented SSC in order to synchronize their team quickly and to set clear expectations from the start. It has also given these physicians a vehicle to get feedback from staff who, feeling intimidated by such an authority figure, would normally choose not to do so.

I have facilitated about one hundred SSC sessions. This powerful process is very effective at surfacing trust issues and work issues within a group. As a manager, I find SSC sessions to be the most efficient and effective way to learn what to do to best develop and improve both individuals and teams. SSC also illuminates what is working well on a team and allows me to support the continuation of that, too.

Freedom is reached
the day you don't
need to be lied to
about anything.

"Accountably
is reached the day
you don't tolerate
being lied to about
anything."
–Don White

PART III

ACCOUNTABLE CONSCIOUSNESS

What It Means to Be Accountably Conscious

- I determine my own life and I am capable of making any changes I wish in myself, in my relationships, and in my work situation.
- Whatever the present moment contains, I accept it as if I had chosen it.
- What I am really choosing in every moment are consequences, some of which I may like and some of which I may not like, but which are not inherently right or wrong, good or bad.
- I am 100% responsible for every experience in my life.
- To become aware of my connection to my experience, I ask myself how I am creating or perpetuating the very situations I claim to not like.
- How I know what I really want is by noticing what I have. All the rest is simply what I say I want.
- Lack of awareness severely limits my choices.
- I assume in any instance that I am doing the best my prevailing awareness allows. I do not blame or fault myself.

What impact would accountable consciousness have on productivity, effectiveness, and morale if everyone in your organization put it into practice?

"The best years of your life are the ones in which you decide your problems are your own. You do not blame them on your parents, the ecology, or the president. You realize you control your own destiny." –Albert Ellis

If you do not intentionally choose account-able consciousness you will suffer the con-sequences of unaccountable consciousness.

With Accountable Consciousness:

"You are energetically alive. People can feel you when you come into a room. When you look at them, they feel seen. When you listen, they feel heard. When you speak, they listen." –Susan Campbell, *Getting Real*

Accountable Communication

Communicating accountably flows from accountable consciousness.

Accountable consciousness is not automatic or self-sustaining. It takes a profound commitment to be self-aware and to be real. There are no handy 1-2-3 steps or progressions; no clever quadrants or diagrams. It is not linear. Accountable Communication Technology offers a way, however, to build and sustain this way of life.

Dye versus Paint

Accountable consciousness works like a dye. It penetrates the whole. Paint is applied to a surface and remains topical. Sooner or later weather and wear will reveal the original surface beneath paint. Not so with a dye. Awareness is like a dye. It is not superficial behavior modification. Awareness is more a fundamental attitude adjustment which results in behavioral transformation. *Awareness is basic to accessing your consciousness.* Nothing changes without awareness. Awareness is a conscious choice. It comes when and only when you call for it. Awareness increases with practice, but it is never fully automatic.

Developing Accountable Relationships

Your team or colleagues can constitute a mutually supportive "recovery" group to help one another move from unaccountable to accountable consciousness. This means each of you '100% responsibility for your relationships. You own the

Here's how: each of you commits to give and receive feedback in the moment when you hear one another using unaccountable language, *especially* in meetings. This works best if you meet as a group and agree to it. It's a business deal because it enhances everyone's productivity. **Be forewarned: as your awareness of unaccountable interactions across your organization heightens you may be staggered by how pervasive they are.** You will also begin to realize how unaccountable interactions blanket our society at large. **The accountable point of view provides a profound insight into why we have the problems we have.** We are immersed in an unaccountable culture. However, you *can* make your workplace an oasis of accountability.

Accountable Language

Unaccountable communication results from unconsciousness. Your words and sentences continually reveal the state of your conscious thought. This is a beautiful thing. Our words and sentences completely and precisely reveal whether we are in an accountable state, or unaccountable state. If you want to become more aware of yourself and practice accountable communication, simply notice what you are saying to yourself and notice what you are saying out loud. Awaken to yourself. Notice in your self-talk and your conversation with others how often you are actually blaming them in some way for your experience.

"Paying attention to your exact words is a portal to presence second to none."
–Don White

For example, consider how unaccountable *and* common the following statements are. Can you turn each into an accountable statement? If so, notice your thinking process. Changing these into accountable statements is a direct experience of the awareness and understanding of accountability.

"You make me feel angry . . . sad . . . happy . . . frightened."
"You make me feel (whatever)" is perhaps the most noticeable and obvious manifestation of a lack of personal accountability

heard 24/7, the world over. It pleads powerless over your state, blaming someone else for feelings you yourself have chosen to have. The accountable statement would be "I'm feeling angry . . . sad . . . happy . . . frightened."

Nobody makes anyone feel anything.

I'm an identical twin. Even though we are cell-for-cell clones of one another, in seemingly the same situation and hearing the same words from our parents at the same moment, we frequently had different feelings and reactions. Identical twins notwithstanding, we always had independent choice.

"You are distracting me."

What is true is that I am *allowing* you to distract me. I am *choosing* to give you my attention. You did not take it from me. I am in charge of and responsible for who and what I do with my attention.

"S/he put me on the spot" or "You're embarrassing me."

No one can "put you on the spot." You are always at choice about feeling pressured or embarrassed, no matter how hard someone tries to "do it" to you. You could simply find the situation interesting or perhaps even funny, but not necessarily stressful. Becoming free of the illusion that anyone or anything can pressure or embarrass you or *make you feel* anything is deeply rewarding and empowering.

"S/he intimidates me."

Accountably speaking, you are allowing them to intimidate you, even if he is your boss or an authority figure of some kind. Other coworkers may not find them intimidating. It's a choice whether or not to be intimidated.

In *Eyes Wide Open*, the author, Isaac Lidsky, says, "I mo̤ experienced pure, unrestrained fear when I learned I was going blind." Lidsky was in his early 20s. But not long after he had the profound realization that he had complete power to determine what it meant to be blind. In fact, he said being blind "opened his eyes"!

> Blindness helped me to see . . . In every moment, we choose how we want to live our lives and who we want to be. This is our ultimate power. Too often we lose sight of it. Most of us never fully understand it.
>
> Your life is not happening to you. You are creating it. Every action you take, every thought you have, every word you utter, your every emotion—at the core of it all is choice. Your choice.
>
> With this empowerment comes complete and inescapable responsibility . . . tell yourself that others control your choices and you are choosing not to choose.
>
> You can live unintentionally. You can exist as reaction, as happenstance. Those are choices you can make. Many people do.

Feeling intimidated is neither good nor bad, right nor wrong; it just has consequences. Most people don't enjoy feeling intimidated. Confronting intimidation has consequences, and not confronting intimidation has consequences. Either way, you are choosing. For example, think of someone in whose presence you once felt intimidated, but now no longer do. Have you ever "had enough" of something and made a different choice about dealing with it? We get what we put up with.

"I notice I am allowing myself to feel intimidated" is to be accountably aware of a *choice*.

"You are subject to your experience, but not at the mercy of it." –Don White

"You can't be honest with most people here."

More accountable would be, "I am not going to be honest with most of the people here," or, "I'm not open with most of the people here."

"I can't make the meeting today" or "I can't do that right now."

We frequently use the word "can't" when what is accurate is "won't." Short of some physical restraint, what's true is that you are choosing to do something else instead for whatever reason. What's true is that you're not going to do x right now. "I'm going to (continue to) work at my desk instead of going to the meeting" would be an accountable statement. To appreciate the importance of this distinction, for one week use the word "won't" where you would normally use "can't." This will heighten your awareness of accountability.

"I didn't have time to call you" or "I didn't have time to get to (whatever)."

"I didn't have time" is a lie. Accountably speaking, I chose to do other things rather than call you. In effect, calling you was not a priority, *but I don't want to say that*. The "I didn't have time" excuse is a classic Usual Agreement: I won't confront you on it if you won't confront me on it. That way we reserve our right to put one another off without being straight about it. "I didn't want to call you" is the truth, and would be the accountable answer if questioned.

"I have to go to work" or "I have to get this report out today."

You don't have to go to work today, or ever. You prefer the

consequences that go with having a job rather than those that go with not having a job. Same with doing anything when on the job. You do what your role requires because you do not want the consequences of not doing them. "I'm going to work" or "I want to get this report out today" are accountable.

"I just can't stop thinking about it."
What is true is that you *won't* stop thinking about it. You are getting something out of obsessing over it.

"Meetings are boring and a waste of my time. The boss always digresses and we never get through the agenda."
No one can bore you or waste your time without your permission. *You get what you put up with.* Boredom happens anytime you choose to withhold about it rather than speak up, then and there, with something like, "I notice I am losing interest in this discussion. I don't see how it relates to the agenda item. I want to return to the point where we were reviewing the specs on the product changes."

Such a non-blaming statement would be said in a factual, not a whiny tone.

Something would happen. Either someone would make a case for furthering the current discussion and its relevance, or the focus would shift per your request.

A Further Problem
There is another problem when thinking and therefore speaking unaccountably and as if a victim: *You are blaming someone*, and that starts trouble.

Recall a recent time that you felt blamed by a coworker (refer to the list of unaccountable statements above to help). Recall how you reacted to the accusation. Did you like the implication that you were the cause of their problem? Very likely you came to your defense, feeling somewhat irritated by the insinuation(s). Suddenly you're on the brink of an unproductive interaction unless you avoid getting defensive.

If you are a "people pleaser" and unwilling to tolerate others becoming angry or upset with you, you will likely be drawn into an elaborate, placating drama, fearing that the friendship is at risk. Such distractions interfere with doing your job.

The Bottom Line

How many of the above described interactions do you suppose happen daily in your company, organization, department, or team? How much time, energy, productivity, and morale are lost annually to unaccountable interactions? Blaming and defending. Blaming and defending. Blaming and defending. On and on and on . . .

"Our lives are not determined by our circumstances. We determine our own lives by our reaction and response to our circumstances."
–Don White

Accountable consciousness awakens you from the common trance of powerlessness and negativity.

The *consciousness* of accountability is energizing and freeing. Incapacitating self-blame is replaced with self-acceptance and compassion, which also quells your inclination to blame others.

Statements Disguised as Questions

Statements disguised as questions, aka "loaded questions," are another very common example of unaccountable language. They reveal unaccountable consciousness. They are manipulative. Pretends. They are cheap shots, disrespectful and negative, and in a way, violent. Also considered "passive aggressive" behavior, they are a common part of The Usual Agreement. Any form of passive-aggressive behavior is unaccountable.

> *The tone of a statement disguised as a question is critical or suspicious, and is* almost always *detected by the listener. The intention of the questioner is everything. 'Why did you do that?' is only a legitimate question when the questioner is actually curious, rather than upset that the person did whatever they did.* –Don White

As children, in our earnest attempt to figure out what adults were saying to us and to avoid trouble, we learned to read between the lines of statements disguised as questions. "You call that clean?" turns out to mean "Your room (clothes, hands, etc.) are *not* what I call clean and you're in trouble." Soon enough, we learn from adults this manipulative, indirect communication technique. By the time we are adults, everyone is doing it and it goes unchallenged for what it really is.

How do you feel when you detect a statement disguised as a question that is directed at you? What do you do? Do you pretend the question is a legitimate question? Do you respond as if it were a statement rather than confront the disguise? How complacent have you become to The Usual Agreement?

Responding from the New Agreement consciousness would be something like saying to the speaker, "'How much longer do you have to wait for the new part to be approved?' sounds to me like a statement. I think you are frustrated that the project deadlines have not been met, and you're not meeting your promises to customers, and you want a completion date that you can count on. I'm wondering how much of what I just said is accurate and complete."

You get what you put up with.

Common Statements Disguised as Questions

Convert each of these questions to the hidden statement within. There can be various ways to express the statements. Example:

"Are you going to do that again?" could be, "I don't want you to do that again" or "I didn't like it the first time you did that. Don't do it anymore."

Do you *really* think that will work?

Don't you think you're being a little *defensive?*

You really think I have a choice in this?

Didn't you know the meeting started at 9:00?

Aren't you ready yet?

How many times do I have to go over this with you?

You really find *that* interesting?

Is *that* the best you can do?

Don't you think you can do better than *that?*

You're not going to quit *now,* are you?

You *really* think that's funny?

Are you really interested in what I am saying?

Are you *listening* to me?

Don't you think I'm right?

Don't you think you are jumping to conclusions?

Is anybody else hot in here?

Don't you think this meeting is boring?

Do you really think this meeting is necessary?

Don't you think that is long overdue?

**Being committed to
The New Agreement,
you unmask
statements disguised
as questions
anytime, anywhere.**

Accountable Conversation

Many years ago, in a shop-talk conversation with Ron Luyet, co-author of *Radical Collaboration* and *The Green Zone*, I asked of all the many techniques for effective communication and relationship building that we use, which one he considered to be the most essential. "Listening. *Really* listening," he responded without hesitation.

Listening is an attitude, not a behavior.

Listening

Never pretend you are willing to listen to someone when in truth you do not want to, either because you don't want to deal with the person just then (or at all) or you want to be doing something that is more important or urgent to you. Accountable Communication requires your full, undivided attention. Therefore, be honest when you don't want to listen to someone and honest about why.

Most of us do not truly listen to one another; we debate, or we wait for "the noise" to stop. We are too occupied thinking about what we want to say back while the other person is still talking, *especially if we think we are being blamed*, talked "at" or talked down to.

Accountable listening reduces blaming and defensiveness, *especially if you do not trust one another*.

To listen accountably means that at *any time* you can tell the speaker what he or she is saying, almost as if you were a recording device. You **do not** offer any of your thoughts, opinions, critique, or analysis of what you have heard. At first, for most of us, this is very difficult to do and feels foreign.

(Note: your turn to get heard will come, but if you want a better chance of getting heard, learn to *listen first*.)

Accountable listening includes noticing what feelings the speaker seems to be having and acknowledging *that* to the speaker, **without** your opinion of the feelings, such as, "You seem irritated" versus "You don't need to get mad."

Conscious, accountable listening is essential to efficient, effective interactions.

Accountable listening does not guarantee you will agree with one another. You will, however, clearly and completely understand each other, where you agree and where you disagree, which is essential to problem solving or finding a resolution.

**Accountable
consciousness
brings forth
heightened presence.
It is a quality of
engagement that
both sees and listens
with the intention
to miss nothing.
Getting real keeps
you present.**

Getting Heard and Understood

Think about getting heard as if you were serving up a meal for someone to eat and you wanted them to taste and digest the food thoroughly, rather than feeling gorged or bloated from eating too much too fast. Furthermore, consider that they may not want to eat right now, or at least what *you* are offering.

Therefore, instead of talking rapidly and non-stop and trying to "sell" them, pause often to check in with your listener(s) by asking something like "I'd like to know what you hear me saying so far . . . " It can be helpful to add something like "I just want to hear what you are hearing, *not* what you think about what I have said so far." Checking in is a way of making sure they have heard what you are saying.

Listen carefully to the response. Usually, people will launch into their opinion or critique of what you have said, or will take your request as an opportunity to talk about themselves or something else. If so, get them back on track by asking what they heard you say. Continue to do so until you are clear that you have been understood.

In all your conversations, you are responsible for the following:

- Being certain that those to whom you are speaking are hearing from you what you want them to hear.
- Being certain they understand your point of view, especially if they do not agree with it.
- Being certain they know how you *feel* about it, if that matters to you.

No one can be unclear about what you are saying or misunderstand you without your allowing it.

The quality, efficiency, and effectiveness of any conversation is determined by how accountably you participate.

Accountable Agreements

The intention of Accountable Agreements is to ensure that we ask for what we want rather than hold back. Most of us really don't expect others to do what they say they will do and won't confront them when they don't. We don't want to deal with the possibility that the other person will be uncomfortable or upset or not like us for being direct and straightforward. But accountable agreements have no place for withholding. (Even attempting to manage their feelings toward us is unaccountable.) The intention is to place you at 100% responsibility for your involvement and not end up a victim of other people's excuses and non-performance.

Accountable Agreements require agreement on the following components:

1. What is to be done
2. Who will do it
3. By when

Accountable Agreements **never** have the following sort of phrases in them: I think it would be a good idea if you . . . Why don't we . . . Maybe you should . . . My suggestion for you would be to . . . I'll try to . . . I'll see about . . . What if we . . . Let's . . . I'll bet we could . . . You might try to . . . I think I can . . . , etc.

The above phrases are musings, general ideas, and suggestions. They characterize a vague, noncommittal discussion, **not** an agreement for action.

Accountable Agreements can be renegotiated to allow for the fact that while we bargain for climate, what we get is weather. Any changes to Who, What, and By When must be mutually agreed upon.

This formula is meant to be applied across the spectrum of your relationships. Do not allow people you think you depend upon, such as coworkers, bosses, suppliers, vendors, subcontractors, customers (internal and external), government employees, members of institutions, family, friends, etc., to be less than 100 percent responsible for their words and actions, which includes what they *don't* say (withhold) as well as *don't* do. End all meetings with a recap of all agreements, or a confirmation that there are no agreements. Consequences for broken agreements include:

- Anger, confrontation, and upset
- Erosion of trust and respect
- Poor performance review; job loss

Triangulation (Backstabbing)

In our company, we refer to Triangulation as 'Third Party Talk'. It is unaccountable behavior, and results in disciplinary action. Failure to end this behavior results in termination.
–Matthew Bernard, CEO, Darex Manufacturing Company

By **triangulation** I mean the act of talking *about* someone with whom you are upset to anyone other than that person—a third person. The fact that you are talking about them means your upset is significant. This behind-the-back gossip goes on all the time, is unaccountable, and absolutely toxic. This underground, backchannel "buzz" causes negative, hurtful stories to start and circulate. The phenomenon is at best distracting and at worst devastating to critical team relationships and trust. It is a source of us-and-them. The third party usually feels pressured to take sides. It is a national pastime. **To stop this alone would transform your organization.**

How to deal with an invitation to triangulate at the workplace

"Venting" does not suffice for or excuse one from accountability. When anyone comes to you complaining about someone else, interrupt the person, acknowledge his or her upset, and ask the following question: "When you said this to him/her, what happened?"

There are only two possible responses to this question:

1. "I didn't tell this to x," or
2. An account of the conversation that took place specifically on this point.

If you get #1, make an agreement with the complainer to tell everything he/she is telling you about the other person *to* the person within 24 hours and report back to you within 24 hours about what happened. In the case of the second response, move into problem solving and/or offer to facilitate a meeting of the two.

The intention here is to support direct, open communication. Be clear with them that you see their upset as a *mutually* created situation in which each person is 100% responsible for the situation *and* the resolution.

You are training people to talk *to* one another rather than about one another; to deal directly with one another rather than avoid one another.

Ray Dalio, founder of the investment company Bridgewater Associates and author of *Principles*, which describes his "Radical Transparency" culture, declares:

> Never say anything about someone that you wouldn't say to them directly . . . there is never a good reason to bad-mouth people behind their backs. It is counterproductive and shows a serious lack of integrity, doesn't yield any beneficial change, and it subverts both the person being bad-mouthed and the environment as a whole. Next to being dishonest, it is the worst thing you can do in our community.

Meetings and Accountability

If you've ever sat in a meeting that was a complete waste of time, you were probably surrounded by people unwilling to speak the truth. —Annette Simmons, *A Safe Place for Dangerous Truths*

With the New Agreement, meetings are always worthwhile. *No one allows them to be otherwise.*

Dr. Schutz's Fundamental Interpersonal Relations Orientation (FIRO) theory dealt with the specific *interpersonal anxieties* related to our sense of significance, competence, and likability. Because most of us regard our lives as a performance and want to be regarded as succeeding, our Image Management Department, fearing public disapproval, has a distracting obsession with other people's judgements and opinions of us. This is especially activated in groups and meetings. Ironically, the very effort to preempt disapproval and appear successful undermines being present, and yet presence is the accountable and anxiety-free state that maximizes effectiveness.

You own the quality of any meeting you find yourself in (and, any conversation you are in, for that matter).

Every meeting is a business meeting and what happens there is your business because it affects you, one way or another. Time and energy will not be squandered—not on your watch. Being comfortable is not in your job description, or in The New Agreement. Commitments to "comfortable" are a constraint on being real.

Seeing and Saying

In meetings, keen discipline is required to be non-defensive and undistracted by our own anxious, incessant mind chatter and to be completely focused and present. Attentive, you sit forward. You are on it. You do not wait for others to make the meeting worth your while. You say what you see when you see it and you say it directly. When fear influences behaviors and actions in the meeting, you address it calmly, compassionately, and effectively—then and there.

Being willing to see the interactions transpiring in front of you, especially defensiveness, is intrinsic to accountability.

Being fully present during an interaction or meeting keeps fears and insecurities from affecting you. You stay on task and on topic, unwilling to wander from the matter at hand or to settle for less. A non-anxious presence has a positive effect on other people. It provides a rare oasis of calm, centered attention that encourages others' participation.

Accountable Participation

Accountable participation means you notice and take action in the moment on the following:

- Defensiveness in any of its forms
- Digressions from agendas and getting off-topic
- When someone is repeating themselves
- When someone is not listening. Check this out by asking what he or she is hearing the other person say.
- When someone is not understanding someone else
- When two people are disagreeing but not acknowledging it
- When someone is withholding
- When someone is pretending
- When someone is blaming or being unaccountable
- When there is unacknowledged fear in the room
- When someone is obviously checked-out
- When someone is talking "for the group"
- When someone is being passive-aggressive

What difference would it make to your organization if everyone in the organization took ownership in this way for every meeting?

Interviewing and Accountable Consciousness

Faced with the apparently daunting prospect of transforming an organization from the well-entrenched Usual Agreement to Accountable Consciousness, the hiring process is usually the last thing that comes to mind. However, nothing is more important than getting the right people to join the company in this effort.

Don White, who conducted interviews throughout his 26 years at Procter & Gamble, offers the following:

> Because the New Agreement stands our traditional conditioning on its head, it is critical that interviewers completely abandon the Usual Agreement hiring process and start over from the New Agreement Accountable Consciousness perspective.
>
> Fundamental to this approach is making the process experiential rather than intellectual. Doing this gives the candidate the opportunity to experience the *feeling* of working in an accountably conscious environment, and gives the interviewer an opportunity to experience the candidate in this environment, all in real time.
>
> The whole feel of the interview process is profoundly different from the process most of us grew up with under the Usual Agreement. Under the Usual Agreement, the

interview process had the candidate working diligently to appear professional and undeniably qualified for the job. Besides researching the hiring company and the job in question, the candidate developed a carefully rehearsed script in anticipation of the standard and most likely interview questions—like preparing for a theatrical performance—the Image Management Department at full tilt. It was the interviewer's responsibility to do everything possible to circumvent this act and find the real person beneath it.

In fact, executive career coaching and job transition training firms regard the interview as a performance, and train their clients "how to act" during the hiring process, then turn around and train the interviewers in companies how to penetrate this very act in order to ascertain how the person behind the act would fit in the company.

With accountable consciousness, gone is the one-up attitude of the interviewer, along with any inclination to *interrogate* the applicant. Also gone is the notion that the candidate is somehow on the spot, at the mercy of the interviewer, and has no real control of the process or the outcome. Regarded accountably, the entire interview process is seen as a collaboration between interviewer and candidate to determine if the company is right for the candidate and the candidate is right for the company.

During the interview process, the interviewer stays open to and conscious of their own *feelings* about the candidate, in addition to their thoughts. This might include "Would I like to work *for* him?" "Does he feel welcoming and approachable or cool and distant?" and

"What kind of energy will this candidate bring to the team and the company?" The interviewer treats their own feelings and instincts about the candidate as data important to the interview process. The idea of a candidate's "energy" being important sometimes draws skepticism from prospective interviewers new to the process. They think of energy as some ephemeral, vague quality beyond their grasp. I advise them that energy is a very real, easily felt phenomenon. I ask them to think of a person who seems to be able to brighten up a whole room simply by leaving! Invariably they smile as a particular face comes to mind. Nothing subtle there. The negative impact on a team or whole organization of a person carrying that kind of energy is profound, but traditionally unappreciated and unaddressed. Notice these people. Don't hire them.

During the interview, the interviewer uses her own experience in living accountably and consciously. There is no script for this and no rigid outline to follow. She might ask questions like:

- What was the biggest failure in your life up until now? How did you react and respond to this?
- How will I know when you're angry with me?
- In what circumstances are you most likely to get defensive?
- What do you like the most about yourself?
- What do you like least about yourself?

The interviewer decides during the interview which of these or other probes are most likely to reveal the real person. At all times during the interview process, the interviewer is open with the candidate about themselves, frequently volunteering their own responses to some of the questions. This serves to provide examples, but also to demonstrate the interviewer's willingness to be vulnerable and less than perfect. The interview is a true two-way conversation and an opportunity for both to develop an accountable relationship.

If you want the candidate to be real with you, get real with the candidate.

Matthew Bernard, CEO of Darex:

I have a handful of questions that I like to ask to get things going.

Here are a few:

- What are you doing right now to get feedback in your job or life?
- Tell me about some feedback you received that you didn't agree with in a previous job
- Do you know exactly what your current or last boss likes most about you, your technical competence, and how you do your job?
- Do you know what they like least?

- ○ Usually the answer is "No." If so, I the "Why not?"
- ○ What could you do to find out?
- What do you like most about yourself?
- What do you like least about yourself?
- What are you most enthusiastic about?
- How will I know you are mad, irritated, upset with me?
  - ○ Give me examples from your past job

The richness comes from digging into and exploring these questions with the applicant. I usually spend about an hour with them, and need only a couple of the above questions to get the conversation moving away from canned answers.

Patty Casebolt, Clinical Director at Medical Eye Center:

Successful recruitment is the first step toward staff retention. We can teach the technical components, but find it very difficult to teach the other qualities necessary to thrive within our unique culture. We are looking for individuals who are uncommonly self-aware, open, and who take full responsibility for themselves and their choices. We explain to candidates that we have a very high-feedback culture and expect staff to give and receive feedback spontaneously as well as participate in frequent feedback sessions. During an interview, we look for a willingness to answer questions honestly, especially when doing so requires not pretending and being non-defensive. No spin.

We expect our interviewers to demonstrate and model this in the interview. If the interviewer is feeling anxious or self-conscious, she will be open about it at the start of the meeting. This is true for group interviews, as well.

Organizational transformation is not complete until the interviewing process is overhauled.

Benefits of Accountable Consciousness

We reclaim our personal power by taking responsibility for our consciousness.

Accountable Consciousness is a path to aliveness, free from the trance and stance of a victim and of defensive living.

Understand, from time to time:
- You will be ignored and excluded.
- Your competence will be questioned and doubted.
- Someone will dislike you.
- You will be mistrusted.
- You will be disrespected.
- You will be blamed.

No problem.

With Accountable Consciousness
- You will get included when you want to be.
- You will be acknowledged as competent when that matters to you.
- You are more likely to be trusted.
- You will never see yourself as a victim.
- Your vitality and self-esteem will flourish.
- You will be heard and understood.
- You can find out where you stand with anyone.

With Accountable Consciousness, you no longer fear people as you did. You have personal resources for your interactions and relationships that were previously unknown to you. You no longer *have to* be seen as significant, competent, and likable because you are not driven by the fear that you are not. Unburdened by maintaining an Image Management Department, you enjoy presence of mind and self-empowerment. Your life is less stressful, more interesting, and more enjoyable. Freedom realized!

Imagine This Characterizes Your Organization

- Conversations and interactions are accountably open.
- Triangulation stops.
- Everyone in every meeting takes 100% responsibility for the quality and effectiveness.
- Employees want to be at work.
- No more Us and Them or We/They.
- Employees are not afraid of their managers.
- Managers are not afraid of their employees.
- Employees take pride in the company and talk it up, not down, to others.
- The Ain't It Awful Club closes for lack of members.
- Cynicism gives way to enthusiasm.
- Defensiveness is regarded as a business cost, not a cost of doing business.

Imagine

An accountably conscious
employee
In an accountably conscious
culture
In an accountably conscious
organization

In an accountably conscious world

Afterword

I began writing *Please Lie to Me* in 2004. In 2005, I became enmeshed in divorce and found myself too distracted to continue with the book. In 2007, the divorce still unresolved, my earlier atrial fibrillation returned with a vengeance and resulted in my having ablative heart surgery. In 2008, due to the economic recession, all eight of my business clients cancelled all work that was scheduled for that year. In 2009, I was back to writing *Please Lie to Me* when I received a diagnosis of aggressive, Stage II prostate cancer. I again suspended writing. I chose to skip conventional treatments. For the next five years I tried dozens of unconventional treatments. Albeit slowed, the cancer progressed.

In 2014, The Mayo Clinic in Minnesota found the cancer had metastasized to Stage IV. The doctor estimated I had two months to a year to live, perhaps a bit longer if I began chemo, radiation, and hormone treatments immediately. But I did not feel desperate. I passed on their offer to undergo what is referred to by cancer patients as "The Ring of Fire."

Back home in Oregon, I soon found myself receiving visits from warm and caring hospice workers who deeply honor this most vulnerable phase of a terminal illness. I began to prepare to die with their guidance and intimate embrace. I found the experience wonderfully "tenderizing" and humbling. A peaceful "letting go" was underway as I entrusted myself to Death.

However, in late 2014 my daughter, Rissa, made a decision that I had not anticipated.

She wanted to continue my work and take over my role in the business. I was thrilled. I asked God for that to happen and to grant me an extension. Now, nothing was more important than to pass on stewardship of ACT consciousness and its future as a business to Rissa. I know the practice of ACT has the power to deal with The Fear Factor. I sensed she knew what she was getting into and had the courage to do it. I could see it in her eyes. If she chose to practice Accountable Consciousness and to make a profession of it as an ACT consultant, what more could I want?

Shortly thereafter, as if in answer to my prayer, a request for extensive ACT work came from a company in Los Angeles. With Rissa at my side I was able to handle the volume of work as well as its providing a perfect mentoring opportunity for us.

As the weeks unfolded I was astonished to witness her almost instant competency as a co-facilitator. Her presence in the room grew daily. In a few weeks, I noticed the participants were making as much eye contact with Rissa as with me, and directing as many questions to her as to me. I felt myself easing back as she stepped forward to take equal responsibility; the handoff was happening. Our connection with one another was becoming seamless and powerful. What a gift I was being given! How grateful I was.

One evening over dinner in LA, I was expressing my surprise and wonderment at Rissa's comprehension and articulation of ACT. I called her a "walk on."

With an amused look on her face, she leaned back in her chair and chuckled.

"Dad," she said, "you trained me in ACT for twenty-seven years!" "No, I didn't," I protested. I went on to explain that I hadn't because she seemed so interested in the fine arts from childhood. In support of my assertion, I pointed out that she ended up with a degree in film and digital media from University of California, Santa Cruz.

I had not sensed in her or her brother any particular interest in pursuing my profession. While Rissa did attend some ACT workshops between middle school and high school, I thought the reasons had to do with specific leadership and student government roles and responsibilities. Even though she attended a few after college, too, I had not realized how interested she actually was in group dynamics and human relations.

"Yeah, I know all that," she responded. "What I mean is you related to me like you do with everybody. Accountability is your life context 24/7. You aren't perfect, but you are consistent. No exemptions and no exceptions. I learned early on it was useless to try to sell you on why I wasn't accountable for stuff. I always knew where I stood with you. No sugar-coating or watering down—as if I needed sheltering from the truth." As I was taking this in, she added, "You always treated me as an equal and as capable of handling my life and of getting whatever I wanted for myself. So, I have twenty-seven years of exposure to ACT, as a matter of fact. Yeah, I get it."

And now I got it. Like children learn their native language, she had osmotically learned accountability. I had taken courses in early child development and family-of-origin psychology in the Holistic Psychology program, but I did not grasp how thoroughly parents imprint their children until this dinner conversation with Rissa.

There was one other event that made our conversation even possible.

Having survived 2014, and wanting to live to see Rissa's declaration come to fruition, over the course of 2015 I submitted to eight surgeries, including orchiectomy, without which I would have died. The medical prognosis at the end of that ordeal was that I had about four more years before the cancer was predicted to reactivate. I now fondly refer to this chapter of my life as "testosterone-free living."

And the prognosis meant one more thing: I had another chance to finish *Please Lie to Me*.

Cancer has enriched my life in the way only a life-threatening illness can. It is a unique stimulus to awareness and freedom. We have Death to thank for our life. To avoid all that Death brings to Life is to miss an indescribably exquisite, divine gift.

I believe I am still alive in order to get this book into your hands. May it stimulate, inspire and persuade you to transform your organization to Accountable Consciousness using Accountable Communication Technology.

Thompson Barton
March 10, 2018

User Experiences

These are comments from leaders who have years of experience using ACT in their companies. These accounts are as much about the user as they are about ACT. All are willing to talk further with you.

Darex Manufacturing Company
Ashland, Oregon

Matthew Bernard, CEO

Founded in 1973, Darex is the maker of the world's best-selling knife and tool sharpeners. Since the late 1990s we have placed within the top 10 "Best Places to Work" in Oregon, and "Best" several times. We sustain this through uncompromising quality in all our manufacturing processes, our values, and our culture. One-third of our employees are directly involved in the assembly of our products. In 2000 we began using ACT. It's a winning combination.

We are as rigorous about Quality Relationships within our entire workforce as we are about our product quality. People issues are addressed immediately, as are technical problems. Employment at Darex is as dependent upon coworkers' relationship skills as it is on their technical skills. We have been using ACT to teach our employees optimal communication skills since 2000. Our Continuous Improvement efforts apply across "people skills" as well as technical competencies. We achieve this with continuous, daily feedback about every aspect of our business, which includes our very intentional, clearly defined culture. Because of our evolved quality of rpersonal communication, we have no need for an HR department. Triangulation, or "Third-party talk,"as we call it, is not allowed. Employees are expected to talk *to* one another rather than about one another when they have difficulties. If they want facilitation, they arrange it. They are equally responsible for the issue and its resolution. Not to do so is unacceptable and a violation of their employment agreement. I, myself, would not work here if the culture were other than accountable. Darex is well known in this area for its outstanding culture of accountability. That is a decided business advantage in a tight labor market like ours.

Expectations at Darex for Sustaining Our Culture

1. No pretending. Notice when you are pretending, which is saying or doing something that is not true for you. Confront pretending in yourself and others, saying exactly what feels true for you.

2. No blaming. Notice where and when you are blaming: yourself, other people, the world.

3. Take responsibility for every experience—you are determining your own life and are capable of making any changes you want in yourself, in your relationships, and in your work situation. Ask yourself: What do you want, what are you planning to do to get it, and what is your next step?

4. At Darex there is no right and wrong, only opinions. There are, however, always consequences of our choices, even our choice of opinions. Talk about what you like and don't like, never what or who is right or wrong. Keep this in mind at all times, with every person, in every situation. Ask others for their opinions. Use "tell me more about that" more than you ever have before.

5. Explain, don't justify. Explaining is about being clear; justifying is about being right. Stop and notice what feels true to you in the moment. Ask others: "What are you hearing me say?" Understanding someone and agreeing with them are two different things, and neither has anything to do with being right.

6. The objective of any conversation is to be able to explain the other person's point of view. Talk about where you agree and disagree, then ask: "Where do we go from here?" Create the next step together.

7. Notice when you are planning what you are going to say, then stop thinking and just say what is true for you. Notice when others are planning their thoughts; call it out, and ask them to just speak what is true for them instead strategizing how not to say what is true for them.

8. Assume you are not being as open and accountable as you think you are. Consider openness and accountability as a journey, not a destination. What will you do next to be more open and accountable?

9. Notice when you are preoccupied thinking about someone. Go tell them what you have not told them; there is something there.

10. Notice how you are training people to treat you in every interaction.

11. Take responsibility for knowing what's going on at all times. When you are not sure what is going on, what the plan is, or what your role is in the plan, go find out.

12. Know where you stand with everyone you interact with. If you don't know, go find out. Knowing what someone thinks about you is 100 percent your responsibility.

James River Corporation
Cincinnati, Ohio

Russ Salzer, Former General Manager

Five years after our location was acquired by a Fortune 200 Manufacturing Company, we were last in every key performance indicator: Safety, quality, productivity, cost reduction, and earnings. If our site could not be turned around, it was going to be shut down. Directly contributing to low performance was misaligned leadership and a non-collaborative culture built on unaccountable confrontation as the main means of communication.

Accountable Communication Technology was applied by the leadership and expanded to the leadership team and gradually to the rest of the plant employees, which included two different labor unions. ACT was used to introduce a culture of openness and personal accountability. Concordant decision-making greatly accelerated buy-in of critical changes on the factory floor as well as with other departments. Plant-wide communication meetings became the norm for an opportunity to practice and apply their techniques—sharing financials, results, and goals.

In less than eighteen months, the site went from last to first in every area.

- Sales: 17 percent increase
- Safety: 92 percent reduction in Lost Time Injuries
- Quality: 25 percent improvement
- Productivity: Up by 25 percent
- Costs: Decreased by 12 percent
- Profit: 11 percent increase; the facility became the most profitable plant in the division

Additionally, the company prided itself on best practices—i.e. not reinventing the wheel—and strongly encouraged shared learnings between sites. When the turnaround was underway, the site became the focus of attention for other facilities to learn from and emulate. Our Accounting Department, for example, figured out how to complete month-end closing 50 percent faster than any other plant across the entire corporation.

Peninsula Light Company
Gig Harbor, Washington

Russ Salzer, Former Director of Operations and Engineering
At the time I joined, Peninsula Light Company was the second largest cooperative utility in the Pacific Northwest.

Numerous issues were facing the company when the transformation work was started. There was little personal accountability. Safety performance was terrible—one in five were injured on the job! Safety is obviously critical for a utility as the jobs of the crew are very high risk. There was a large amount of fear and mistrust between union/operations and salary personnel. Not only were there challenges between union members and staff, but also contention and divisiveness between the water and electrical divisions. The utility entered the water business seven years prior and had not become self-sufficient and was being subsidized by the electrical side.

The transformation began with the management team by establishing a more collaborative, open standard of operating focused on specific performance improvement. Accountable Communication Technology was used, and all department leaders were trained and given the tools required for organizational transformation. The work focused on developing a new culture, one that was made up of high inclusion, accountability, and results. Once leadership momentum was established, the balance of the organization was trained in ACT. Soon, company-wide communication meetings began with the open sharing of results, something that was quite foreign prior. Additionally, not long into turnaround, the culture had been transformed to one of highly collaborative problem solving, peer-to-peer performance reviews, salaried staff spending time in the field, and much more fun. In just sixteen months the following great results flowed:

- Safety: Best on record with a 50 percent improvement
- Engineering: 22 percent performance increase
- Operations: 60 percent performance increase
- Income: Reversed the negative earnings trend, and the water department became self-sufficient and provided funds for much-needed capital improvements
- Costs: $1,000,000 improvement
- Culture: Unification between work groups improved dramatically

Medical Eye Center
Medford, Oregon

Paul Jorizzo, M.D. Managing Partner

Seventeen years ago, our medical practice had much in common with many small businesses. We suffered from lack of trust and had conflict at the partnership level. Managers were frustrated and their discontent trickled down throughout the organization. Partners avoided one another, and their associated teams were embroiled in a web of triangulation and competition. Unable to achieve consensus, our practice stalled. After several failed attempts with conventional consultants I was resigned to a future of dysfunction, but our new, creative administrator convinced us to try something different, called Accountable Communication Technology.

Introducing us to ACT was a pivotal moment both personally and professionally.

For me it was liberating to realize that we are all imperfect. I became aware of how futile it is to try to hide my flaws. Being more open seemed beneficial both at home and at work. Our partnership conflicts initially remained, but we felt more empowered to resolve them. We officially embraced accountable communication as the standard and expectation for our relationships at MEC. All employees were given the opportunity to leave or remain and support the transformation. A few did leave, but that left us with enthusiastic commitment and an immediate improvement in morale. We extending ACT training to managers and then staff. We became more efficient, and the joy of work was returning.

Since that time, we have continued our quest to achieve and maintain our accountable culture. Patients frequently say that our office has a different and positive vibe. Before new doctors and staff are hired, they are informed that accountability is an essential part of our culture and our expectations. Almost universally, applicants are enthusiastic about participating. Many employees have been with us for more than a decade. As we add new doctors, and senior doctors approach retirement, our staff has voiced concerns that accountable communication principles and training may not continue. But, at our annual doctor and manager retreat, I was filled with pride to witness all forty-seven attendees openly discussing the importance of sustaining our special culture as well as expressing appreciation for its contribution to their lives.

John Welling, MD

As a first-year surgeon at this practice, I can't say enough about the positive impact of ACT on the work environment. Having just emerged from ten years of training at various academic centers, and having witnessed firsthand the significant fallout (and sometimes complete implosion) caused by fear, withholding, and unresolved interpersonal conflicts, the contrast couldn't be clearer. I now work in an extremely supportive environment where every employee is trained, invited, and encouraged to be completely open and accountable—from the front desk staff to the most senior surgeon. ACT equips and empowers every employee in the practice to give and receive feedback, solve their own problems, and take responsibility for their own success and happiness. There's no way to place a value on the problems avoided and the productivity gained.

Burke Williams Spas
Los Angeles, California

Bill Armour, Owner and President

In the thirty years that Burke Williams has been in business, the conscious implementation of ACT principles as a core value in our business has been the decision that most improved business efficiencies. At its core, accountable communication has elevated the quality and efficiency of interactions between employees and thus our ability to adapt and respond rather than maneuver.

My first ACT experience was with our seven-member core team. At that time, without any awareness, we were immersed in professional jealousies, fear, and defensiveness. Decisions that could have been made in minutes were taking days as we maneuvered around each other's feelings and agendas— trusting no one.

Immediately after ACT our communication began transforming. We each understood the value of openness and self-awareness, and the cost to us and to the business of our defensiveness. We committed to accountability and accountable relationships. This wasn't the usual pablum of patting each other on the back as a mask to cover real issues. This was an altogether new, very intentional business process. With its adoption, a new era has dawned in which trust is treated as an essential business asset, and fear is treated as a liability.

Whether owner, management, or font-line worker, applying ACT will transform your organization at every level.

Recommended Reading

In nearly forty years of work as a business consultant and facilitator focused on accountable consciousness, I have found a few books that are helpful in dealing with fear and building trusting relationships and workgroups.

Susan Campbell, PhD. *Getting Real: 10 Truth Skills You Need to Live an Authentic Life.* Novato, CA: H J Kramer Book & New World Library, 2001.

This book teaches a set of communication and awareness practices that anyone with a sincere desire for better relationships can apply in their daily lives. In a sense, it's a book about how we can use our daily life experiences to become more honest, self-aware, and resilient—by applying Campbell's 10 Truth Skills. But first we have to come to terms with all the ways we have been conditioned to look good, appear in control, and manage the outcome of our communications so that no one gets too uncomfortable. *Getting Real* is a practice for helping the reader "get comfortable with normal discomforts of adult relationships," learning to work consciously with our resistances to what life offers us—so we can "relate" to life realistically rather than trying to "control" life to fit within our comfort zone.

Susan Campbell, PhD. *Saying What's Real: 7 Keys to Authentic Communication and Relationship Success*. Novato, CA: H J Kramer Book & New World Library, 2005.

Susan is world-class in the area of relationship consciousness. This book de-mystifies the process of being completely honest by introducing seven simple phrases that immediately bring your interactions into present time. Instead of getting caught up in old communication patterns (such as the need to justify, explain, or impress), the seven keys will make it easy to say what you really feel, think, and want with clarity and presence. This book is a primer for becoming a more conscious, courageous, and loving human being.

Kathleen D. Ryan & Daniel Oestreich. *The Courageous Messenger: How to Successfully Speak Up at Work*. San Francisco: Jossey-Bass Inc., 1996.

This book is about what it takes to reach personal transformation in the work place and how to leverage that toward creating a more open, less fear-driven organization. Great inspiration is found in these pages as well as the practical "how to." This book was long overdue in the organizational development literature in 1996 and is still ahead of its time.

Kathleen D. Ryan & Daniel Oestreich. *Driving Fear Out of the Workplace*. San Francisco: Jossey-Bass Inc., 1998.

The title is true to the focus of this book. I have yet to find a book that deals so thoroughly with the impact fear has in the workplace, why fear reigns, and why leaders do not deal with it. Ryan and Oestreich quantify fear as the liability it is. The cat's out of the bag with their work. I admire the authors for not shying away from this very unpopular subject in the field of organizational development. Fear seems to be the last dysfunction business leaders are willing to deal with.

...ᴜᴏᴜᴇ makes this book courageous. "How to" is implied in this book's title, and it does a fine job of guiding that undertaking.

Robert Kegan and Lisa Laskow Lahey. *An Everyone Culture: Becoming a Deliberately Developmental Organization*. Boston: Harvard Business Review Press, 2016.
An in-depth, encouraging account of the evolution of Bridgewater Associates, The Decurion Corporation, and Next Jump, Inc., toward increasingly conscious cultures and the rewards thereof. It is heartening that after thirty-four years, Schutz's *The Truth Option* begins to surface.

Will Schutz, PhD. *The Truth Option: A Practical Technology for Human Affairs*. Berkeley: Ten Speed Press, 1984.
In the mid-1960s, at the height of a very successful career in academia, Dr. Schutz did a trust-fall into the open arms of the Human Potential Movement. This is a workbook that covers the combination of self-awareness, self-disclosure, and self-responsibility that, when practiced, will transform your life. This book introduces the reader to the FIRO theory, which identifies the three basic dimensions of human behavior that are at play when we have relationship issues anywhere in our lives.

Jim Tamm and Ron Luyet. *Radical Collaboration: Five Essential Skills to Overcome Defensiveness and Build Successful Relationships*. New York: Harper Collins, 2004.
Defensive behavior is the most pervasive interpersonal problem getting in the way of effective collaboration. This book focuses on easy-to-learn skills that help readers overcome defensiveness and become more successful at collaboration.

Related Reading

Alasko, Carl. *Beyond Blame*. New York, NY: Penguin Group, 2011.

Beal, Danna. *The Tragedy in the Workplace*. Spokane, WA: Destiny Publications, 2001.

Bechtle, Mike, MD. *Dealing with the Elephant in the Room*. Grand Rapids, MI: Baker Publishing Group, 2017.

Britten, Rhonda. *Fearless Living*. New York, NY: Penguin Group, 2001.

Campbell, Susan. *From Chaos to Confidence: Survival Strategies for the New Workplace*. New York: Simon & Schuster, 1995.

Connors, Roger, Tom Smith, Craig Hickman. *The Oz Principle: Getting Results through Individual and Organizational Accountability*. Paramus, NJ: Prentice Hall Press, 1994.

Connors, Roger and Tom Smith. *The Journey to The Emerald City*. Paramus, NJ: Prentice Hall, 1999.

Cooper, Robert K, PhD, and Ayman Sawaf. *Executive EQ: Emotional Intelligence in Leadership and Organizations*. New York: Berkley Publishing Group, 1996.

Covey, Stephen. *The Speed of Trust. The One Thing That Changes Everything*. New York: Free Press, 2006.

DeSteno, David, PhD. *The Truth about Trust: How It Determines Success in Life, Love, Learning, and More*. New York: Plume, 2014.

Dyer, Wayne, PhD. *Excuses Begone! How to Change Lifelong, Self-Defeating Thinking Habits*. Australia: Hay House, 2009.

Ekman, Paul. *Telling Lies: Clues to Deceit in the Marketplace, Politics, and Marriage*. New York: W.W. Norton Company, Inc., 2009.

Eurich, Tasha. *Insight: Why We're Not as Self-aware as We Think, and How Seeing Ourselves Clearly Helps Us Succeed at Work and in Life*. New York: Crown Business, 2017.

Feldman, Robert. *The Liar in Your Life*. New York: Hachette Book Group, 2009.

Gallwey, Timothy W. *The Inner Game of Work*. New York: Random House, 2000.

Gladwell, Malcolm. *Blink: The Power of Thinking Without Thinking*. New York: Back Bay Books, 2005.

Glasser, William M.D. *Choice Theory: A New Psychology of Personal Freedom*. New York: HarperCollins Publishers, 1998.

Goleman, Daniel. *Emotional Intelligence: Why it can matter more than IQ*. New York: Bantam Books, 1995.

Goleman, Daniel. *Vital Lies, Simple Truths: The Psychology of Self-Deception*. New York: Touchstone, Simon & Schuster, Inc., 1985.

Hallstein, Richard W. *Memoirs of a Recovering Autocrat: Revealing Insights for Managing the Autocrat in All of Us*. San Francisco: Berrett-Koehler Publishers, Inc., 1992.

Johnson, Larry & Bob Phillips. *Absolute Honesty: Building Corporate Culture that Values Straight Talk and Rewards Integrity*. New York: AMACOM, 2003.

Lencioni, Patrick. *The Five Dysfunctions of a Team: A Leadership Fable*. San Francisco: Jossey-Bass, 2002

Lidsky, Isaac. *Eyes Wide Open: Overcoming Obstacles and Recognizing Opportunities in a World That Can't See Clearly*. New York: TarcherPerigee, 2017.

Marshall, Edward M. *Transforming the Way We Work: The Power of the Collaborative Workplace*. New York: AMACOM, 1995.

McKay, Matthew, PhD, and Patrick Fanning. *Self-Esteem: A Proven Program of Cognitive Techniques for Assessing, Improving, and Maintaining Your Self-Esteem* (Fourth Edition). Oakland, CA: New Harbinger Publications, Inc., 2016.

Miller, John G. *QBQ! The Question behind the Question: Practicing Personal Accountability in Business and in Life.* Denver, CO: Denver Press, 2001.

Patterson, James and Peter Kim. *The Day America Told the Truth.* New York: Plume, Penguin Group, 1992.

Rabbin, Robert. *Igniting the Soul at Work: A Mandate for Mystics.* Revised Edition. Charlottesville, VA: Hampton Roads Publishing Company, Inc., 2002.

Rieger, Tom. *Breaking the Fear Barrier: How Fear Destroys Companies from the Inside Out and What to Do about It.* New York: Gallup Press, 2011.

Schaef, Anne Wilson and Diane Fassel. *The Addictive Organization: Why We Overwork, Cover Up, Pick Up the Pieces, Please the Boss and Perpetuate Sick Organizations.* New York: Harper & Row, 1988.

Schutz, Will. *The Human Element: Productivity, Self-Esteem, and the Bottom Line.* San Francisco: Jossey-Bass Inc., 1994.

Scott, Kim. *Radical Candor: Be a Kick-Ass Boss without Losing Your Humanity.* New York: St. Martin's Press, 2017.

Scott, Susan. *Fierce Conversations: Achieving Success at Work & in Life, One Conversation at a Time.* New York: The Berkley Publishing Group, 2002.

Secretan, Lance H K. *Reclaiming Higher Ground.* New York: McGraw-Hill, 1997.

Simmons, Annette. *A Safe Place for Dangerous Truths: Using Dialogue to Overcome Fear and Distrust at Work.* New York: AMACOM, 1999.

Smith, David Livingstone. *Why We Lie: The Evolutionary*

Roots of Deception and the Unconscious Mind. New York: St. Martin's Press, 2004.

Tapscott, Don and David Ticoll. *The Naked Corporation: How the Age of Transparency Will Revolutionize Business.* New York: Free Press, 2003.

Welch, Jack, with Suzy Welch. *Winning.* New York: Harper Collins Publishers, Inc., 2005.

Acknowledgments

Without the help and support of my business partner, Don White, I would not have attempted to write this book. Because he lives Accountable Consciousness, his comprehension is profound. To have co-facilitated with Don since 1991 has been deeply rewarding and enlightening. I am so grateful for his contribution to my life.

Many thanks to Ron Luyet, Keith Casebolt, Randy Johnson, and Bobak Farzin for continually reviewing the manuscript with me.

The financial support of Bruce and Kim Raskin allowed me to weather the 2008 recession and begin the writing of *Please Lie to Me*. Had I not gotten as far along as I did that year, I think being diagnosed with cancer in 2009 would have dissuaded me from restarting this undertaking in 2017.

I thank Ryan Walsh for his classical guitar music, which became my auditory companion all day long for twelve months. His two CDs played continuously, yet I never tired of it. Mysterious.

Thanks to my copy editor, Jenny Meadows, whose thirty-three years of involvement with More To Life made her uniquely suited to grasp the nature and intent of *Please Lie to Me*. Her contribution was beyond technical. I'm grateful to Warren Kahn, author and Senior Trainer with More To Life, who introduced me to Jenny.

Thanks to all of you who have encouraged me to write this book ever since Don and I began offering ACT workshops. I certainly would not have undertaken the project without your support and continued interest in its dissemination.

The Authors

THOMPSON BARTON was raised in Little Rock, Arkansas. As a thirteen-year-old, he witnessed the contentious integration of Central High School in 1957. The fear and the resulting behaviors aroused by the civil rights movement in the South left him deeply disturbed as well as fascinated, haunted by the questions it raised: "Why are we so afraid of one another?" and "Why are we so mean to one another?"

Barton attended Rhodes College in Memphis, Tennessee. As a student, he began to realize that the answer to his questions about human beings required serious self-inquiry as well. The focus of his quest turned from why are *they* frightened to noticing his *own* fears and judgments.

During this time, Martin Luther King Jr. was murdered in downtown Memphis and the Vietnam War was raging. Barton's initial plans for law school faded as an interest in the education field continued to grow. In 1967 he began teaching at a rural high school in Missouri.

In 1968, Barton participated in his first "encounter group," led by Huston Smith, the scholar of world religions from MIT. The three-day experience was profound and illuminating. Barton knew he had found his path, and that self-awareness was the portal. The encounter group called for a transparency that was as foreign to him as it was deeply compelling. From that point on, he began "feeling" his way along in life rather than engineering a career. He chose to trust his calling and pursue what fed his sense of aliveness and curiosity about fear in our lives.

In 1970, Barton cofounded a small manufacturing business that continues to thrive. In 1982, he received an M.A. in Holistic Psychology from Antioch University West, San Francisco, California. From 1986-1989 he was a trainer and consultant in the San Francisco office of Drake Beam Morin, Inc., an organizational development firm. In 1990 he worked as a course designer and trainer for SportsMind, Inc., a firm that specialized in team building. In 1991 he co-founded Barton White Associates with Don White.

DON WHITE, a 1963 Naval Academy graduate, joined Procter & Gamble's manufacturing division in 1967. During his 26-year career at the Baltimore soap plant, he held nearly every management position in the plant, both line and staff. This was a time of transition for the 50-year-old plant. This traditionally managed plant was struggling to compete with P&G's newer, high-performance, non-union facilities. In the course of leading this transition, Don discovered material developed by Dr. Will Schutz, an eminent psychologist, designed to develop individuals and teams in organizations. This material and the associated applications proved pivotal in turning the plant from a traditional, highly conflicted, rigidly structured factory with marginal results into a high-performance plant which competed successfully with the best of P&G's newer, non-union facilities. Don used his remaining years at P&G to spread the technology that had proved so successful in Baltimore to other P&G locations, and in 1990 he began consulting with Thompson Barton. In 1993 he retired from P&G and joined Barton White Associates, Inc. full time.

Our clients have included: The Coca-Cola Company, Dial Corporation, Procter & Gamble, Shell Oil Company, James River Corporation, Fort James Corporation, Ivex Packaging

Corporation, Microsoft, Mini-Grip/Zip-Pak, Drill Doctor, Barcodes West, Printpack, Rexam Metallizing, Garlock Sealing Technologies, Multicolor Corporation, Barclay Dean Construction, Allpak Container, Rhinelander Paper Company, Raytheon Aircraft Company, Raytheon Aircraft Service, and Packaging Dynamics Corporation.

In addition to providing initial training in Accountable Communication Technology workshops, Don provides follow-up coaching at all levels in the organizations, from the CEO to the hourly teams.

Contact Us

In this book, we have offered you the heart and soul (consciousness) of Accountability as we know it after thirty-seven years of facilitating ACT workshops and consulting to business organizations.

For organizations wanting to create and grow a culture based on The New Agreement, we offer a five-day experience in a workshop format. Please contact us with your questions about ACT, our workshops, and speaking engagements.

Practicing Accountable Communication Technology Develops Accountable Consciousness

tjb@pleaselietome.com
www.pleaselietome.com
www.act.biz
Tel: 541-600-2141